SHOULD I
FORGIVE?

RAPE, TORTURE, MURDER - THE ORDEAL OF A
WOMAN WHO DEFIED MUGABE'S THUGS IN ZIMBABWE

NYASHA 'MANY FACES' GAPA

SHOULD I FORGIVE?

RAPE, TORTURE, MURDER - THE ORDEAL OF A
WOMAN WHO DEFIED MUGABE'S THUGS IN ZIMBABWE

MEMOIRS

Cirencester

Published by Memoirs

MEMOIRS
PUBLISHING

25 Market Place, Cirencester, Gloucestershire, GL7 2NX
info@memoirsbooks.co.uk www.memoirspublishing.com

First published in England, February 2013

Book jacket design Ray Lipscombe

ISBN 9781909544253

Printed in England

This book is dedicated to all the innocent souls who have been raped, tortured or murdered during the political violence in Zimbabwe and xenophobic attacks in South Africa. It has been written in memory of those who suffered, including Farai Kujirichita, Kapfudza Tafirenyika, Douglas Mutesa, Costan Musariri, Kasambarare Mariseni, Katsande Clever, Kazemba Alex, Knight Ngoni, Maramba Rosemary, Nyarai (who bled to death after being gang raped and vaginally mutilated by Zanu PF militia), Lunga Edna (abducted, tortured and burnt with plastics), Mavhangira Pepukai, Mabwera Brighton, (four years old, burnt to death while sleeping in his parents' home), Machasi Maxwell, Machipisa Elliot and Madamombe Nguwani, just to mention a few.

We remember you. We mourn you and we salute you.
May your souls rest in peace.

ACKNOWLEDGEMENTS

A huge thank you to my friends at Wordszilla, Erika Potter, Luis Bonilla and Kristin Smith for all your support. Kristin, thanks for all your help in making *Should I Forgive?* better than it started out.

A big thank you also to my online family, the talented staff and writers at writing.co.uk, particularly Lorna Read and Jane Buckley for their encouragement, assessment and inspiration.

INTRODUCTION

Most people in Zimbabwe were looking forward to our country's elections in March 2008. This was the year we believed President Robert Mugabe would finally bid farewell to the presidency. The elections were expected to be Mugabe's toughest electoral challenge yet - Zimbabwe's dreadful economic situation had, it appeared, put an end to his chances of political survival.

My husband Peter and I, as dedicated loyalists of the opposition party MDC (Movement for Democratic Change), had worked very hard to bring more members to our party, as we wished to see the tyrant's rule come to an end. We were fully convinced that the time for change had come, for we were tired of the empty promises Mugabe was constantly giving as he pretended to listen to his people's concerns. Life for us had become a nightmare because of him, and fighting for change was the only way forward.

It had all started in 2000, when the Mugabe régime embarked on a controversial fast-track land reform programme. This had begun in part about twenty years earlier, when Mugabe had worked with the United Kingdom on the land distribution programme, which was intended to correct the inequitable land distribution created during the colonial era.

This aggressive move by Mugabe resulted in an economic downturn in Zimbabwe. The United States put a credit freeze on the country which wiped out our trade surplus, causing it to go from an excess in 2000 to a deficit which has increased every year since.

Other problems arose. As the élite families began taking over land once cultivated by experienced farmers, the food production greatly decreased, causing the supply to drop drastically and spreading famine and starvation.

Mugabe's policies were condemned both at home and abroad, yet his heart remained iron hard. He continued giving to his supporters and taking away from those who opposed him. Consequently, a wide range of sanctions were imposed against Mugabe, the individuals and companies who associated with him and the government of Zimbabwe.

As a result, Zimbabwe was gripped by record-breaking hyperinflation, bringing international media attention to the country. Mugabe vehemently opposed this, as he wanted to keep his actions as contained as possible.

Efforts to hide the hunger and starvation of the masses from the media were escalated by the brutal treatment of opposition members and mass arrests of journalists, not to mention refusing to allow foreign journalists into the country. This era marked the dawn of Mugabe's 'vampire' attacks as he preyed on his own masses to satisfy his political thirst and hunger.

The people of the once proud capital and Africa's breadbasket were plunged into a horrific struggle as their country became the African hunger dungeon. Many citizens were reduced to pedlars, paupers, hawkers and black market hustlers, consuming at most a meal a day to energize their tortured minds, their hollowed cheeks, protruding jaws and sharply-defined ribs were a clear testament to their starvation.

To add salt to the excruciating and bleeding wound, cash dwindled in all quarters. For many, banks became a thing of the past. Instead of customers flowing in and out of the thriving banks, the empty buildings now had the homeless sleeping outside the cashless buildings, while empty ATMs hung uselessly on the walls.

Economists predicted that the only way to rescue Zimbabwe from the mouth of the lion was to change the leadership. With Robert Mugabe's hands removed from the control of the economy, the country could recover. While we all hoped he would resign, this was more of a dream, as he would never consider such an action; we knew the only way to be free was for him to be voted out of power.

This prompted countless Zimbabweans to join the opposition party, led by Morgan Tsvangirai, who was taunted and branded 'Chematama' ('big cheeks') by Mugabe and his fanatics. My husband and I had joined the MDC party in 2005, as it had been formed on the basis of relieving the struggle of the people, creating and providing jobs, establishing decency, justice, transparency and democracy in government, providing equal distribution of resources and maintaining equality among all Zimbabweans. With this platform, the MDC became the light of hope in the gloom. It was the only party which offered the hope of giving the men and women of Zimbabwe their rights back.

After the elections, which were described as peaceful and a credible expression of the will of the people of Zimbabwe, we eagerly awaited the announcement of the key to our freedom. But alas, no official results were announced. It took more than a month for the sad truth to dawn upon us. Mugabe had cheated once more. He had destroyed the key to our democracy. He refused to release the results. This failure to discharge the results was strongly criticized by the MDC leadership, which successfully sought an order from the High Court to compel their release.

After a recount and verification of the results, the Zimbabwe Electoral Commission announced, on May 2 2008, that Tsvangirai had won 47.9

percent and Mugabe 43.2 percent, thereby necessitating a run off, which was to be held on June 27. The pronouncement of a re-run revived a hope which had become comatose, and this time around we were convinced there would be no escape for this tyrant and his régime.

Despite Tsvangirai's repeated claims that he had won an outright majority, he decided to participate in the second round, presumably to prove his claim. By April we had already started hearing rumours of the possibility of this second round. I, my husband, and our campaign team then began to work on tactics to win over those who had voted for Robert Mugabe in the first round in case the rumours were true. The attacks described in this book started on April 19, before the results were announced.

CHAPTER I

'Daddy! Daddy! Daddy!' our daughter Sheila screamed with excitement. She had been helping me to gather firewood, but she sprinted away from me when she saw her father, Peter.

I looked up and smiled as I watched my tired husband drag his feet behind our four cows, a small fortune to us. He was wearing his favourite blue overalls, rubber rain boots and an African sisal hat to shield his face from the scorching Murehwa sun. *Here comes the most handsome man in Nyamutumbu village,* I thought.

'Daddy!' she delivered her final scream as she jumped full force onto Peter's brawny chest. 'My little angel!' Peter exclaimed with delight, swinging her around.

A warm feeling of happiness filled my heart as I heard my five-year-old girl giggling with excitement. She loved her father to bits. He was her favourite, which, immature as it may sound, made me feel jealous at times.

She was the best thing that had ever happened to us, the source of our joy and happiness. It was such a blessing to have such a lively and beautiful little girl around, giving us so much love. She was constantly smiling and full of energy; that is how I always described her.

I had eagerly watched my daughter's progress throughout

her short life, anticipating every inch of growth and each new developmental milestone. It made me feel so good to see some of my physical characteristics in her, with a bit of Peter in her as well. Looking at her, it was as if I were looking at a picture of myself as a child. She had my round face and my long, thick hair. I could see her developing big hips and a round backside when she was grown up. I hoped she would develop that way - Peter said that was what had caught his eye when he first saw me. That didn't make me too happy. While I felt I was by far the most beautiful girl in our village (an opinion echoed by the numerous boys who were after me), I thought Peter would be swept away by my blue, lazy, sexy eyes, my luscious long hair, my beautiful pointed nose and my lovely chocolate skin. For him to say that only my hips and big backside caught his eye was disappointing at first. Eventually, however, I came to embrace what Peter loved about me.

Within a few months of giving birth to Sheila I had regained my beautiful figure, thanks to my house chores, which were as good as working out in a gym. Women in rural areas, I've noticed, are quite fit compared to our counterparts in cities, as we are required to do more physical labour. We walk long distances every day, fetching water and helping with the hard work in the fields.

The only attributes Sheila had got from Peter were his brown eyes, big ears (which seemed to be running away from his head) and his light complexion.

We had talked about trying for a second child. It had always been my dream that Sheila would have a sibling. We had decided to wait, nervous about our financial situation, but

Peter and I finally felt the time was right. I had scheduled a hospital appointment to get the hormone implant removed by the doctor. I knew my husband would be over the moon if God blessed us with a baby boy this time. I always imagine my husband weaving through the Nyamutumbu Mountains with Peter Junior by his side, showing him the 1,000 year old cave paintings and the different trees and bushes that evenly covered the vast Murehwa forests. I imagined him showing our son the different leaves used to cure many ailments and teaching him how to hunt and fish - essential skills for a young man growing up in the rural areas.

Our cows were now used to the order of the day and I looked on as they walked straight towards their kraal. The sunlight was fading, creating new shadows around the cows as they walked away. Ahead of them near their kraal, trees lashed and crashed against each other as numerous monkeys jumped up and down on the branches. They blurted out hostile screeches, as if to intimidate the cows not to go into the kraal.

Peter walked towards me with Sheila still in his arms. This was very unusual of him, as he would usually secure the kraal before he came to greet me. I had a feeling something must have gone wrong.

That week of April 21 2008, it was the beginning of our turn to look after all the cattle in the whole village. It was a hard and painful task for a single person to do and in most cases the cows would go astray and some would end up in other people's fields. There was a weekly rotational duty to look after the village cattle and this was our week. I couldn't wait for it to be over.

'Daddy! What did you bring me today?' asked the still excited Sheila.

'I didn't manage to bring you anything today, love. I'm so sorry,' replied Peter. 'The cattle gave me a hard time today. They didn't give me time to get your favourite fruits.'

'Uh!' she grimaced.

'Sheila, your father is tired, please give him a rest. He will bring you the fruits tomorrow,' I said, trying to comfort her.

He put Sheila down, grabbed me, and gave me a kiss. This was odd behaviour for my husband. I couldn't even remember the last time he had kissed me. This kiss was different from any other I could remember. It was long and passionate.

We loved each other dearly, but we believed public displays of affection, like kissing, were part of English culture: a culture which I believed had polluted our generation. Now women were putting on trousers and demanding equality with men. We preferred to be traditional in our approach rather than copying other people's cultures. Peter was the head in our family and I gave him the respect he deserved.

Sheila quickly covered her face. She had never seen us kissing and was embarrassed to see it. Shyness was one of the things she surely had inherited from me. I looked down, embarrassed as usual, trying to avoid eye contact with my husband. I didn't want to show him that he had just aroused something in me.

'How was your day?' I asked, hoping to cool down the romantic atmosphere which Peter had just created.

'Hard, as usual,' he replied, looking at me mischievously.

'Tomorrow we will have to come and give you a hand,' I

said as I knelt down to pick up the sticks I was gathering for firewood.

'Don't tell me you are only going to start cooking now' said my tired husband. 'I'm starving!'

'I have already prepared the stew. I'm going to prepare *sadza* [thickened maize porridge] now. I just wanted to make sure it would still be hot when you had it.'

We both laughed as we looked at our daughter, who was still covering her face.

'Like mother like daughter' retorted my husband, smiling.

'No, no, this is too much!' I replied, still giggling.

'That is exactly what you did the day I told you I loved you,' my husband reminded me. 'Then you said 'I love you too' and you ran away.'

'Please, please, let's not talk about that,' I begged, hoping he would stop. The memories of that day made me feel silly and stupid. But he was also forgetting that he had almost uprooted all the grass nearby as he struggled to utter those three words.

'I'm going to close the kraal,' said my husband as he started to walk away.

'Daddy, can I come with you?' asked Sheila smiling.

'You are more than welcome, if you are really up for it. Let's go,' replied Peter. 'Just don't laugh at me when I fall down.'

She smiled and nodded her head in agreement, knowing that she would definitely laugh if her father fell down. What Sheila enjoyed most about helping at the kraal was watching her father running after the calf. The calf was quick and clever, which caused Peter to stumble in most cases.

This was challenging work at times for Peter. It was important that the calf stayed away from its mother at night so that we would have enough milk for ourselves in the morning, then the calf could be allowed to suckle from its mother. But actually getting hold of the calf and putting it away wasn't an easy job, especially for someone who had spent the whole day working outside.

The two walked towards the kraal, leaving me to finish what I was doing. I had to hurry. I had prepared his favourite stew of oxtail mixed with green vegetables. It wouldn't take me long to cook the *sadza*. I wanted my hungry and tired husband to find food ready when he finished locking up the kraal. I knew what it was like, herding close to fifty cattle on your own. The cattle acted as if they knew you were alone on that day and would be even more uncooperative. They knew how to wind people up. They had driven me to tears the last time I had done it myself. The things you don't want them to do and the directions you don't want them to take are exactly what they will do. When I tried to retrieve the ones who had gone astray, I came back to find the others already in someone else's field. And the penalty for allowing that to happen wasn't something to joke about. That was up to the chief of the village, and in many cases he had ruled that cows be paid as compensation. So staying alert and tracking the cows was of the utmost importance.

I had gone into a forest very close to our house to gather the last pieces of firewood I would need to prepare the food. I quickly tied the sticks of firewood together and put them on top of my head, walking as fast as I could, then went straight into our kitchen and started to prepare the *sadza*. After a few minutes, I heard my daughter giggling outside and knew they had finished locking up the kraal.

'Go to your mum, I'm coming. I just want to change out of these dirty clothes,' I heard my husband say to Sheila.

He went to the bedroom to change and she joined me in the kitchen. I could hear him whistling in our small bedroom. I looked at my daughter as she tried to rub off a stain she had got on her new white dress while helping Peter. Though we rarely bought ourselves new clothes, we made sure Sheila always had the best. She took off her new white trainers and sat down next to me.

'So tell me, did he fall down?' I asked.

'Please, don't tell him I told you,' whispered my daughter as she started giggling.

'I promise I won't say a word,' I assured her.

'He fell three times,' said my daughter, laughing louder.

Seeing my daughter's mischievous face, I couldn't help laughing as well.

'But you promised you were not going to laugh!'

'I know, but I couldn't help it. It was so funny Mum!'

I heard my husband singing inside our small bedroom. We had managed to build two huts; one was the kitchen and the other we used as our bedroom. We hoped to build another one, if we managed to have a better harvest this season. Every night, I prayed for enough rain to fall. A drought, aside from preventing us from expanding our home, would have dire consequences for our family. It would force Peter to go to the capital, Harare, to look for a job. The last time he had been forced to find work, I had felt lonely and scared, living alone. Homes in Murehwa were very far from each other and separated by huge fields and mountains, so that even if you screamed for help, your neighbours would be unlikely to hear you.

Five years before, just after we were married, we had had a severe drought. Peter had gone to Harare in search of a job. I was so scared of living all by myself. We had just discovered I was pregnant. While this made it more difficult for Peter to leave, I was just as scared for him to go. I couldn't handle being on a farm with no one else close by, so I had gone to live with his parents a few kilometres away. Murehwa is just 80 kilometres from Harare, so Peter visited as often as he could. Each time he visited, he brought groceries to make sure I had enough to eat. We were one of the few lucky families who could get food, as many suffered. We all depended on our small-scale farm produce to sustain our families. But we all tried to help each other as well; that was always the spirit of the united Nyamutumbu villagers.

Nyamutumbu was a very big village, but we all knew each other by name and were there for each other during weddings, funerals and any hardships that presented themselves to the residents in our village. Even the white farmers around our village chipped in.

Six months after Peter began working in the city, his contract ended and he came back, to my joy and relief, as I gave birth to Sheila days later. It was as if he had brought the rains with him. Since then, we had never had a drought as severe as that one. But a new challenge appeared shortly after which posed more threats than the drought ever brought us.

It all started with the land seizures from the white farmers by Mugabe's regime. The white farmers who lived around our village were like our brothers and sisters. They were involved in all our activities and assisted us whenever we needed help. We were not happy when the land seizures started, as the white farmers were forced to leave. Yet there were a few greedy people in our village who took advantage of the seizures and became the proud owners of the farms.

In 1980 it was Mugabe himself who had preached reconciliation and forgiveness, but years later he was causing appalling pain and heartache. After the land seizures, things went from bad to worse. Food became scarce, as the new farmers didn't have the skills for large-scale farming.

By 2008 we were anxious to see change. We felt we had been robbed in the first presidential elections in March as they were delaying the release of the election results, and were determined to make sure that Mugabe would lose if there was going to be a second round as was being rumoured. Our party was growing stronger every day and we had continued pushing to win more members to our party.

We grew nervous, though, when we heard rumours of political violence in Harare and heard that some of our party members had been brutally beaten and even murdered. We tried not to let such news bother us. In Nyamutumbu, we were like one family; we were united despite belonging to different parties. I was sure there was nothing anyone could do to make us turn against each other.

I looked up and watched as my husband joined us in the kitchen. He had taken off his hat, revealing his shiny bald head and oval face. He was wearing his brown pyjamas and slippers.

'Nyasha, do you need a hand?' my husband asked. I looked up, taken aback. Hearing my first name from Peter sounded queer to me, as I had last heard that name about five years ago. Ever since I had had Sheila, Peter and my family had started calling me *Amai* Sheila (Sheila's mother). What he had just done reminded me of those romantic times when we had been boyfriend and girlfriend.

'*Baba* Sheila [Sheila's daddy], you know it's not good for Sheila to know my first name,' I said as I pushed more wood into the fire.

'Nyasha!' Sheila called out, giggling.

'You see what you have done now *Baba* Sheila?' I said, eyeing him wryly.

'Stop it, Sheila!' said Peter. 'I am the only one allowed to call your mother by that name.'

He came to where I was kneeling, wrapped his hands around my wrists and pulled me up. We were standing next to each other, face to face, before I realized what he was trying to do. I pulled away from him as he tried to kiss me.

'*Baba* Sheila, not in front of our daughter, please!' I said as I pushed him away.

Sheila had already covered her face, but I could see her eyes peeping through her fingers, obviously eager to see what her father was up to. Peter was very strong. He pulled me back into his arms. His mouth claimed mine in a kiss that was sweet and complete. I was shocked, pulling back.

'Oh my God! What on earth has gotten into you *Baba* Sheila? Have you taken *vuka vuka* [African Viagra]?' I asked, pretending I didn't like what he was doing.

While I enjoyed every bit of it, I also felt that it was improper to do such things in front of children. When the kiss finally ended, he continued to hold me tightly against his toned, muscular body. Regardless of my concern for what Sheila saw, it was like a dream. I wondered what had taken over my husband.

'I love you Nyasha,' he said, breathing hard.

I didn't know what to say; shyness took over me again. I couldn't remember the last time he had said that. I knew he loved me very much, but we were not very vocal about it.

'*Baba* Sheila, the food is now getting burnt,' I said as I smelled the burning *sadza*. For a while, we had forgotten that we had a pot on the fire. He released me from his arms and went to sit next to Sheila. I wondered what it was going to be like later in the evening with him in this mood.

'Sheila, you can open your eyes now,' he said as he stroked her hair.

I figured that all his antics were a result of the couples' retreat we had just come from. The retreat had started on Friday April 18 2008 and we had come back the previous night, Sunday April 20. We had gone straight to Peter's parents, where we had left Sheila. That night we had both been so tired that we hadn't bothered practising the skills we had been taught at the retreat. There was a lot we had been taught, at times together as couples and at times separately. Peter had already started his romantic antics, but I was reserving mine for when Sheila was asleep.

I planned to make it one of the best nights of our lives and make Peter gnash his teeth with pleasure. When Sheila was asleep, I wanted to drag him outside to do things he would never forget the rest of his life.

'Excuse me,' I said as I stood up.

'What do you want? I can get it for you,' said Peter.

'I am going to get another candle. You can rest, I know what it's like looking after those wild cows by yourself.' I reached for the door.

I was glad that my husband had not protested. I didn't just want to get the candle, but to start the preparations for what I had planned for him tonight. I walked into our bedroom, took the candle and took off my red underwear. I walked out, smiling as I thought of how my husband would react to finding me not wearing anything under my long skirt.

You think you are the only one who is sexually creative today, Peter? Wait until you see what I have for you tonight. Tonight, I will take the lead. I will be in control and you will see a side of Nyasha you have never seen before. You will write down this day in your diary as a day you will never forget.

CHAPTER 2

I dished out the food, still playing out in my head the things I had in store for my husband. We gathered around to eat and, as always, Peter and I ate from the same plate. This made us feel close to each other. At times, we would end up feeding each other.

'Sheila, can you bless the food please?' I asked after we had finished washing our hands.

'God, we thank you for the food which is in front of us. Bless it and also bless the hands that have cooked the food. Amen,' she finished, praying as I had taught her.

'Amen!' Peter and I replied, like a choir.

'How about the hands that have worked hard to get this food?' commented Peter, wiggling his eyebrows in a teasing gesture.

She closed her eyes and prayed again.

'God, bless my father who works hard every day so that we can eat.'

'Thank you. That's my girl,' said Peter.

'You are very clever, just like your mother,' I said as I started eating.

'No. just like your father,' said Peter, trying to start a playful argument, which I didn't have the energy for.

We looked at each other and smiled, neither of us continuing the playful banter. Talking while eating was taboo in our house, so we all ate quietly. It allowed us time to think over the day. The peace, however, was broken by the sound of singing from outside, though it sounded very far from our house.

'Did you hear of any funeral around today?' asked Peter, looking surprised.

'No, there were none that I know of,' I replied as I stopped chewing to try and listen clearly to what they were singing about.

The sound was definitely from a distance, but seemed to be coming towards our house. We waited a couple of minutes, eating in silence, listening to the singing. After about five minutes, the singing was closer, becoming loud and clear. They were singing praises for President Mugabe.

'Did you hear of any Zanu PF rallies?' asked my concerned husband.

'No, unless something was planned when we were away,' I said as I resumed eating.

'It sounds like the singers are coming here,' said Peter, who had already stopped eating, worried about the chants he heard coming towards our house.

I stopped eating as well. After a few more minutes, it became clear that the people had now reached our land and, from the song, they were clearly supporters of the ruling Zanu PF party. They also knew we weren't Zanu PF supporters. I grew anxious, fearing what this was all about and why they had decided to come to our house singing. At the top of their voices, they sang the fear-inducing words:

'Nyika yedu vaMugabe ndivo vanotonga.
Nyika yedu, nyika yedu yeZimbabwe.
Nyika yedu vaMugabe ndivo vanotonga.
Nyika yedu, nyika yedu yeZimbabwe.
KuHarare he-eemhamha.
VaMugabe ndivo vanotonga.
KuChegutu he-eemhamha.
VaMugabe ndivo vanotonga.
KuMasvingo he-eemhamha.
VaMugabe ndivo vanotonga.
KwaMurehwa he-eemhamha.
VaMugabe ndivo vanotonga.
KwaNyamutumbu he-eemhamha .
Zanu PF ndiyoinotonga.'

'Our country, Mugabe is the one ruling.
Our country, our country Zimbabwe.
Our country, Mugabe is the one ruling.
Our country, our country Zimbabwe.
In Harare he-ee mother.
Mugabe is the one ruling.
In Chegutu he-ee mother.
Mugabe is the one ruling.
In Masvingo he-ee mother.
Mugabe is the one ruling.
In Murehwa he-ee mother.
Mugabe is the one ruling.
Here in Nyamutumbu he-ee mother.
Zanu PF is the one ruling.'

'Sheila, go and hide behind those maize sacks!' I shouted. Hearing myself speak, I was surprised by the tremor in my voice as fear had so quickly gripped me.

'Hurry up!' shouted Peter, also scared. 'Don't come out until we have come back.'

'If we don't come back, stay there until morning and go to Grandpa's place as soon as the sun rises. We will come and get you there,' I said, but my instructions were interrupted by a banging at the door.

'Who is it!?' asked my shaking husband.

'Don't ask us silly questions! Come out now!' barked a husky male voice. They quickly changed the song, singing:

'Chenjera chenjera
Chenjera chenjera
Vanamukoma vanorova
Chenjera chenjera.
Vanorova nemaoko
Chenjera chenjera
Tsvangirai chenjerai
Chenjera chenjera
Mutengesi chenjera
Chenjera chenjera
Vanamukoma vanorova
Vanorova nezvamboko.'

'Beware, beware
Watch out, watch out
Big brothers beat up sellouts

Beware, beware
They beat up with their hands
Watch out, watch out
Watch out Tsvangirai
Watch out, watch out
Sell outs beware
Beware, beware
Big brothers beat up sellouts
They whip with *sjamboks*.'

My husband was the first one to get out of the door and I followed behind. Before we could register who was at our door, Peter was greeted with a ferocious punch, sending him reeling to the ground. It was Adamson - a young man in our village we had helped so many times before - who had hit my husband. I screamed with terror as I saw him crumple to the ground, but before I had even closed my mouth, I was whacked hard on the back of my head. I staggered and fell to the ground by my husband's legs. I didn't see who had hit me. I could hardly see anything because my vision was dark and blurry.

I blinked repeatedly, willing my vision to clear. Once I could see more clearly, I looked around and recognized everyone who was there except two ugly, dark, strong men. One of the men had a freckled face, one eye that was red, and a bald head. He was wearing a pair of blue jeans and a white Zanu PF T-shirt with Mugabe's photo printed on the front. The other one was darker with red piercing eyes, a deep scar down his right cheek, and two front teeth missing. He had a goatee and dreadlocks, and was wearing a blue shirt with khaki trousers. The rest were neighbours and people I thought were our friends. The shock at seeing them was overwhelming. I wondered what they had taken or been given to start behaving in such a horrible manner.

I breathed in hard and smelled a strong stench of alcohol and marijuana. *Maybe this is what is making them behave like this*, I thought to myself. *Why else would they attack their friends?*

'Burn the house! Burn the house! Burn the house!' chanted Paidamoyo Zengeya, an old ugly woman who lived a few miles away.

I gasped. Terror gripped me as I thought of Sheila. I prayed she had stayed away from the house. I began shaking at the thought of my daughter burning alive. Sadness crept into me as well as memories of all the happy moments in our house, of Peter and Sheila's laughter just an hour ago. I glared menacingly at Paidamoyo. I knew I shouldn't be surprised by her chants. She had always been bitter towards us. Peter had told me that she had declared war on him after he had refused to marry her daughter. This, however, seemed like harsh payback.

I looked on as Fanuel, a well-known chain smoker, searched his pockets in search of a box of matches. I thought of Sheila possibly hiding indoors. They were going to burn my daughter! I couldn't let them do that. My mind was racing on the course of action I would have to take in order to save her.

I tried to find a way to escape, to distract them from what they were hoping to do. When I looked at Peter, he was holding his face in one of his hands where he had been hit. He looked back at me and gave me the same look of determination I had. We were together on this. We would do everything we could to protect Sheila.

'Who has taken my box of matches?' barked Fanuel.

I glanced back at him, praying that they wouldn't find the matches.

'You left them where you were sitting!' said Martin, another youth who lived about three houses from us.

'Does anyone else have a lighter?' barked Paidamoyo.

She really was determined to have our house burned down. With her long nails, yellow teeth, wrinkled face and black dress, she looked like a real witch.

'We don't have the whole day, let's get moving,' barked the bald man.

I was relieved. My daughter was safe, at least for now. I was glad that Sheila didn't cry or make any noise. Who knows what would have happened to her if they had found her? I was surprised and glad Paidamoyo did not mention her to the two men.

I wondered who these two strangers were. They seemed to be in charge of everything. There was no doubt in my mind that these men were some of Mugabe's militia who had been sent to inflict terror in our village. I wondered why our friends and neighbours had allowed these two clearly evil men to manipulate them like this. What had they been given to do such terrible things to their neighbours and friends, people they had known their entire lives?

We were dragged to our feet and forced to walk while the group continued with their songs of praise for Mugabe, slapping us in the face at will along the way. My heart was torn into pieces as I heard my husband, with a swollen face and blood gushing out from his nose, crying with pain as they slapped repeatedly where they had hit him before.

From the first time I had met Peter until now, I had never seen him shed tears. Even when he had lost one of his closest sisters, he had put on a brave face. His family seemed to feel the same way. Instead of mourning his sister's death, the rest of the family had decided to celebrate the life of their daughter, which she had instructed them to do before her death from cancer. Now, seeing him cry in pain, I felt a deep sense of sadness for my husband.

We continued to be treated like punchbags until we reached Nyamutumbu Primary School. After walking up the old, wooden stairs, we were led down a small hallway to one of the rooms. As they pushed us inside, we saw some of our active party members sitting around the room. Among the group was Edwin Matavire, our party chairman, and his wife Ruramai. Next to him were Brighton Mamombe, our party organizer, and his wife Chiwoniso. Chiwoniso was my best friend and their six-year-old daughter, Esther, was my daughter's best friend.

I looked around and saw the swollen faces of Titus Nhira and his wife Happiness, Tafara Kaseke and his wife Zvanyadza, Wellington Maseko, a bachelor, and Gertrude Mabika, a widower. Their faces said it all. They had all been brutally beaten and were scared to death.

'Tie them up!' ordered the bald man. He was obviously in charge of the operation. The youths of our village did as they were instructed. They tied our hands and legs, not looking into our faces. Whether it was because of guilt or a lack of concern, I couldn't tell.

'Adamson and Fadzi, bring that new lady to the office,' said the dreadlocked man.

Adamson and Fadzi grabbed me and started dragging me away. I began fighting back, pressing my heels into the floor, trying to stop them from pulling me away.

'Stop! Stop! Please Adamson, Fadzi, let me stay with Peter. Please!'

Is this the last time I am going to see my husband and daughter? I thought, as I struggled against the men's grip on my arms

'Where are you taking my wife? Hey, leave my wife alone!' screamed Peter, struggling against the ropes tied on his wrists and ankles.

'Start on him,' said the leader. 'He has a big mouth like his father, Tsvangirai. Show him what we do to the children of traitors.'

'No!' I shouted, desperation thick in my voice.

Adamson and Fadzi continued pulling me away as I strained my neck to see what was happening to my husband.

I could hear the screams of agony as they began their work. I couldn't see exactly what they were doing; the men had created a semi-circle that blocked my view of Peter. I couldn't bear the thought that they might kill him. The pleas for mercy I shouted as I was dragged to the other room did nothing. They continued pulling me along as I fought them with every ounce of strength I had.

It wasn't until they got me into the other room that my fear and worry for Peter shifted when I saw what was in the classroom. There were four tables put together with an old, rough mattress thrown on top of them. I knew exactly what awaited me. It was clear to me what this office was being used for and I suspected that all my female friends had been subjected to the same ordeal I was about to go through. I screamed in terror and threw my body back, away from the bed. Fadzi's grip on my arm faltered, causing my elbow to hit him in the nose. He released me and grabbed his nose as blood began pouring out.

'You stupid bitch!' he shouted, grabbing a cloth. Adamson seized both my arms tightly, sending pain shooting up my shoulders. He spun me around to face him, glaring at me, an evil smirk crossing his face.

'You'll pay for that! Your precious husband won't want you once we're done. Of course, there may be nothing left of him either.'

He threw me like a bag of garbage onto the bed. I fought against his grip, but some of the other men had come around to help hold me down. I could hardly move.

It's better to die than to go through this. Peter would want to know what they did to me. How am I going to explain this to him? Will he ever want me again? God, what have I done to deserve this?

'Take off her panties!' commanded the bald man as he unbuckled his trousers' belt. 'Let's fuck the pussy of Tsvangirai's bitch.'

I tried to scream, to alert anyone that could help me. Adamson covered my mouth with his hand.

Fadzi flipped my skirt up, revealing everything.

'This one is a real bitch! She's not even wearing any panties!' screamed Fadzi with excitement.

'You must be joking,' said the dreadlocked man.

'I'm not joking, come and see for yourself,' said Fadzi.

I lay there helpless, feeling humiliated as they laughed, looking at my private parts.

'She knew we were coming and decided to get ready for us,' said the dreadlocked man, making everyone burst into laughter.

I tried lashing out, to get away, but it was no use. Some of the men held my arms down while others pulled my legs apart. The leader of the group descended. I felt the mattress move as he came closer, excitement spreading across his face. I shrieked as I felt him force his way into me. I struggled, but soon stopped. I closed my eyes knowing there was nothing I could do at this point to rescue myself from these animals. He thrust in and out forcefully, causing me horrible pain. I screamed in agony as he did it over and over, but Adamson continued to cover my mouth with his hand, muffling any sound. I felt tears begin to drip down my face as the man continued.

I had never experienced anything like this. Peter had always been gentle and loving to me. He never allowed me to feel pain. But this was pain unlike anything I had ever known. I felt everything leave me—my cleanliness, my reputation, Peter's desire to have me. It was all gone. Those I loved would never look at me in the same way again. I would never look at myself in the same way again.

Finally, the leader was done. He stood up and moved to the side, pulling up his trousers. The men continued holding my arms down and pulled my legs apart as they each took turns raping me. The man with the dreadlocks was next, followed by seven other youths from our village, including some we had helped in the past during drought seasons. I viewed them like my own brothers and I felt bile rise up in my throat as they each took their turn with me. There was no look of compassion in their eyes, only hatred and satisfaction.

You are hurting me, please stop. Am I not like a sister to you? Have I ever done anything wrong to you? I thought, the tears streaming down my face. *Oh God, let me die! I want to die, take my life now, Lord.*

When the last man had finished, they pulled me to a sitting position and tied my wrists. They led me back to where others were sitting. I could barely walk, I was so sore. The men holding my arms had to hold me up as I stumbled into the room.

CHAPTER 3

When we entered the room, I froze in place. They were still beating Peter. They were beating him with dried wooden sticks under his feet and buttocks. For a moment, the physical pain I felt was displaced with the anguish I felt for my husband.

I'm sorry Peter. I'm sorry. I know you must have guessed what they did to me. I'm so sorry, but what could I have done? There were too many of them. I feel so helpless now. I understand if you don't want me any more. I can't blame you, Peter. We may not even survive the night. Please forgive me.

'Adamson and Fadzi, you two stay here and teach all these traitors a lesson they will never forget,' said the leader. 'The rest of you, follow me. We have a few more people we need to get.'

I panicked, wondering who they were going to go after now. *What if they pass through our house and hear my little girl sobbing?* I thought. *Lord, please keep these monsters away from my daughter.*

The men beating Peter threw him onto the ground and I was pushed down next to him. I put my tied hands on his shoulders as he rolled on the ground, moaning in horrible pain. Adamson and Fadzi took some beer cans and started drinking as the others followed their leader to get more MDC supporters. We all wondered who was going to be the next victim to be beaten. Fadzi took the wooden sticks and looked at us. I couldn't believe this was the Fadzi I had known since I had moved to Nyamutumbu. It looked as if he was possessed by an evil spirit. His eyes were raging with anger and hatred. They were black and void of any kindness.

'I want you all to sing this song. Whoever does not sing with all his heart will be the first to get the beating,' said Fadzi.

He started to sing and we all joined in, afraid of what he and Adamson may do.

'Nhasi ndapfidza, handichazvipamhezve
MDC ndakuramba nhasi, handichakuda
VaMugabe huyai mutonge, Zimbabwe ndeyenyu
Chiuyai baba VaMugabe, tinokudai.'

'I have had enough today, I will not do it again
MDC I divorce you today, I no longer want you
President Mugabe, come now and rule, Zimbabwe is yours
Come now President Mugabe, we love you.'

We all sang about repenting of supporting MDC and praised President Mugabe except Peter, who was too badly hurt. He could only vaguely mutter the words. I sang, but couldn't focus on the words. I feared for my husband, who was horribly injured. I also worried about my daughter. Never in my life had I left the poor girl by herself. *What is she thinking right now? She must be terrified. Is she worried that she will never see us again?*

'Louder and with passion!' screamed Adamson.

'And why is this one not singing?' asked Fadzi, looking at my husband.

I began shaking with fear and moved my body to block Peter who tried to say something, but before he had finished, they pushed me aside forcefully and were on him again, beating him recklessly all over his body. Again and again, they beat him like a snake, hitting him with their fists, kicking him with their feet, and smacking him repeatedly with sticks. Everyone stopped singing as we looked on in horror.

I sobbed, begging them to stop hurting my husband. He looked close to death. *They are going to kill him. How will I explain to Sheila what happened to her dad? Did she hear our screams when we were being beaten outside our house? Did she hear her dad crying like a little boy? What could be going through her mind right now? If we don't make it out alive tonight, how will she survive without us? Please, someone help us!*

'Keep singing! Whoever stops will be next,' shouted Adamson.

The ordeal was too painful for me to watch. I closed my eyes and prayed for God to intervene. I sang with my mouth, but my heart was saying a silent prayer for my husband. I had no idea how we would get out of this. *We are going to die*, I thought. *We are going to die. Who is going to look after my lovely daughter?* My prayers were answered almost immediately when a car drove into the school, interrupting the beatings.

'Stop singing!' shouted Fadzi.

'Who could that be?' asked the worried Adamson.

'I don't know,' replied Fadzi. 'Let's go and check.'

We watched as Adamson and Fadzi walked out of the building. We could hear them talking to whoever was in the car, but they were speaking too quietly for us to hear. I remained seated, dazed by what had just happened to me and Peter in such a short amount of time.

My husband tried to get up but failed, and I looked in his direction. Blood was everywhere.

'Don't move,' I whispered. 'You're too badly injured. You'll just get beaten more.'

Without responding, he crawled to where I was sitting and broke the ropes on my wrists with his teeth. I was the first person to get free, rubbing my wrists. I looked at Peter, who was staring at my forearm. A bruise had developed in the perfect shape of a man's hand. I looked away, ashamed. Peter took my hand and squeezed it gently. When I looked at him, I saw compassion in his eyes. I felt my chest tighten. I wanted to fall into his arms and have him hold me, protect me, make me feel like myself. I wanted him to make me feel like the person I was just a few hours before.

Peter stared intently into my eyes, focusing my attention on his words.

'Quickly, untie the others before they come back,' said my brave husband.

I worked as fast as I could as we all listened closely to the men outside. They were speaking more loudly now, apparently laughing and joking. As I freed one person, they would then free someone else. Within a short period of time, everyone was free, but no one knew what to do.

'You have to get out of this place now!' said Peter.

'What about you?' asked the worried Brighton.

'I will try to follow, but I can hardly move. Don't wait for me. Don't help me. You'll never make it if you do. If I don't make it, please take good care of my family,' replied Peter.

'No, no Peter!' I whimpered, moving to his side.

'But where will we go?' said Edwin. 'They know where we live, they will definitely come after us.'

'Let's hurry to our homes; if you are willing to risk it, get whatever we need and meet at Mount Chitombosvipa,' suggested Titus. 'From there we will plan what to do.'

'Come on, let's get going now, before they return,' said Tafara.

Everyone got up quickly, leaving as quietly as possible through the door and down the stairs, sprinting away from the school. But I couldn't leave my husband behind. He tried to walk but failed. Slowly, he crawled away from the school with me beside him.

How could all the men sprint away without thinking of helping Peter? I thought bitterly.

Peter stopped once we were a short distance from the school. 'Nyasha, please go, I will be fine,' begged my distraught husband.

'No! I'm not leaving you here by yourself,' I said defiantly, standing my ground.

'If these people catch us, no one knows what they will do to us. I'll only slow us down.' Peter said between breaths, gasping for air as he started crawling again, grimacing through the pain. 'You're the only chance Sheila has. Please go, for her sake,' said Peter.

I knew he was right. I needed to get to Sheila as quickly as possible. But I couldn't help but wonder what Peter would think. If I left him by himself, would he not see it as abandonment? I knew if he were in my shoes, he would never abandon me here by myself. But would I want him to stay to help me, or save our daughter?

'No. We are going to do this together. We are going to make it and we will both be there for Sheila. There is no way I'm leaving you here, not like this,' I said.

'Please, just go!' my husband replied, a look of desperate frustration on his face.

I thought of what he was saying. He was right, for surely if we were caught and killed there would be no one to look after our beautiful daughter. But at the same time, it didn't feel right for me to leave my husband alone in the state he was in. Conflicting thoughts filled my head. *He is right, but isn't leaving him also wrong? Sheila is scared and desperate for me to come back and make her feel safe again. She needs me, but Peter also needs me. Should I go? Should I stay? Oh God help me, I don't know what to do.* Before I could decide whether to protect our daughter or leave my injured husband, I heard Adamson and Fadzi swearing.

'Those bastards have escaped,' wailed Adamson as he slammed the door open.

'We are in trouble. They will think we let them go on purpose' cried Fadzi.

'We have to find them! Come on, let's go,' I heard Adamson exclaim, his voice full of anger.

I could hear their footsteps as they came towards us. I was scared. I could see that there was no way my husband was going to make it. He couldn't move fast enough, and the closest trees he could hide behind were too far. I didn't know what to do. I tried to run, but my legs were numb with fear. I looked at Peter. His face was covered in blood. He was crying, his tears streaking the blood.

'Go! Go Nyasha, please! Go and take care of Sheila. Tell her I love her,' begged my husband.

'Peter, you are with me in my thoughts and prayers. We will conquer this. I love you, no matter what,' I whispered.

I wanted to say more. I knew this could be our last moment together. But Adamson and Fadzi were already nearby. It was too late for me to run far or say anything. I tore my gaze away from Peter and jumped behind a nearby bush, hiding myself. In daylight, the bush wouldn't have hidden me, but I hoped the darkness would conceal me as I crouched as small as I could. It was too dark for me to see what tree I had hidden behind, but the strange potato-like smell revealed it was a potatobush, *Phyllanthus reticulatus*.

'Here is one of them,' said Adamson as he got to where my husband was lying. I could hear the anger dripping through each word. I closed my eyes as they jumped on his back, tramping and kicking him like a football. I forced my fist into my mouth, biting on my hand as I suppressed the screams that were attempting to escape. Even though I didn't see the rest of the beatings, I could hear the groans of my husband as each hit and kick made contact with his body.

'Is he dead?' asked Adamson.

I moved slowly, glancing through the leaves in the bush. I saw them looking down at my husband, who wasn't moving.

I felt myself longing to jump up, to be by his side, to check whether he was dead or alive. It took all of my willpower to stay where I was. *No!* I thought, praying with all of my might. *God, tell me this is not happening. Tell me it's a dream. Wake me up from this dream, Lord. I don't want to lose my husband. I can't leave without him. He can't be dead, no! Lord, this is too much for me to bear. Lord, please help me.*

'No. I think he has just fainted,' replied Fadzi.

'Are you sure?' asked the worried Adamson.

'I don't know,' replied Fadzi, shrugging with apparent indifference.

'Let's just drag him back then,' said Adamson.

I looked on as they dragged my unconscious husband back to the school. I was distraught; I didn't know whether he was alive or dead. His last words came to my mind; he had told me to look after our daughter. Images of the happy moments when Peter had come back from cattle herding flashed before me. I couldn't imagine my life without him. He was my soulmate and I loved him with my entire being. I thought of his gestures of love before we were attacked. I thought of what I had planned to do for him. To think that he could be dead ripped my heart into pieces. The pain I felt was beyond description. He was my other half. My life was interwoven in his. His happiness was my happiness. His sorrow was my sorrow. If he were dead, what was left of me?

I fought hard against the tears that were about to overwhelm me, but I didn't have the strength to stop them. My body was shaking as I sobbed, sitting there in the dark, empty jungle.

CHAPTER 4

I cried for only a moment before getting the strength I needed to stop. Sheila needed me. I needed to be strong for her sake. I needed to get to her before these animals of Mugabe got to her. I picked myself up, staying crouched down and watching the school, making sure I wasn't seen. Once I was sure they could no longer see me if they looked out of the school, I ran as hard as I could to our house to get Sheila. My legs and groin were horribly sore, but I forced myself to run as fast as I could, fighting through the burning pain. When I got to the house, out of breath, I found her still hiding behind the sacks of maize, just as we had instructed her. I was more grateful at that moment than at any other that she was a very obedient girl.

'Sheila! Sheila! It is Mummy, you can come out now,' I whispered as I walked close to where she was hiding.

She came out, shaking and full of tears. She obviously had overheard our screams when we were first taken outside our house.

'I'm so scared, Mum, I'm so scared,' she sobbed.

'Don't worry, I am here now and I won't allow anything to happen to you,' I said as I took her into my arms.

Her small head nuzzled into my neck. I failed to hold back my tears of happiness for our reunion, grief for my husband,

and sorrow for what was done to me. We sobbed for a while together, scared for the future. I held her tightly for a while. She eventually pulled herself back and looked into my tear-filled eyes.

'Where is Daddy?' she asked, worry written across her face.

I wiped the tears from my eyes, knowing I needed to avoid her question in order for us to move as quickly as possible.

'Listen, we have to get going now, there are people waiting for us,'

'Is Daddy waiting there as well?' she asked, showing me she was not satisfied with my answer.

'Your dad wants us to get out of this place for a while, OK? He knows where we are going. He will come and join us later,' I said as I took her hand and pulled her out of the house.

I have lied to my daughter, but how long will the excuses last? What am I going to say to her if her dad fails to turn up? She won't be satisfied with my answer for long.

I went into the bedroom, took a few essentials, including some money, and headed towards Mount Chitombosvipa. We walked as fast as we could, jumping at moving shadows, fear still gripping us.

When we arrived at Mount Chitombosvipa, everyone was already there, pacing up and down as they impatiently waited for us. Everyone was still shaken. Wellington was a distance from the others, wearing blue jeans, a white sweater, and smoking a cigarette. He was obviously trying to calm his nerves.

'Where is Peter?' asked Edwin.

I didn't reply. They all watched me and then bowed their

heads, understanding flowing through the gesture. I remained silent, not wanting my daughter to know what happened to her father, that there was a possibility she would never see him alive again.

'We have decided to go to South Africa. We are no longer safe in this country,' said Titus, moving to the centre of the group. He seemed to have taken the role of leader on our mission to freedom.

I wasn't surprised by this. The Shona custom was that we listen to our elders and let them lead in everything, as we value their experience. Titus, being the oldest, had no choice. He had to live up to the challenge.

'South Africa!' I exclaimed. 'That's too far. How are we going to get there? Don't tell me we are going to walk!' I said as I looked around at the determined faces that had already made up their minds on what we were going to do. It was clear they were not going to allow anyone or anything to stop them on this mission.

How can you be so willing to leave? I thought, as I took in each of their expressions of determination. *It's easy for, you have your partners with you. How can I go that far without knowing Peter's fate?*

'We don't have much choice my dear, and time is not on our side' explained Titus. 'Those men could be out searching for us right now, for all we know. If we stay, we risk being captured again, and very likely killed. We have to do this step by step and see what each day will bring. If we get another form of transport, then all praises to the most high God. But for now, we have to use what we have, which, unfortunately, is our legs.'

'Why South Africa? Why don't we go to Mozambique or Zambia? They're both closer.'

'Most of our party members have fled there. It will be much easier for us to get the assistance we need, plus I have heard there are plenty of jobs down there. We have more options what work we can do there compared to Zambia or Mozambique,' replied Titus.

'How sure are you about that?'

'Gertrude has a brother there. What would he gain in misleading his sister?' Brighton chimed in.

I knew he was right. We had to get out of Nyamutumbu village as quickly as possible. And South Africa would provide us sanctuary from the political turmoil we were escaping. I wanted to wait for Peter, but I knew he would want me to get Sheila away from all the dangers in Nyamutumbu. I hoped Peter would understand my actions. I hoped he knew I loved him.

'So how many days, roughly, do you think it will take to get to South Africa?' I asked.

'Honestly speaking, I don't know, but during the liberation struggle, it took us about a month to get to Mozambique. Though I was young and full of energy then,' replied Titus.

'I didn't know you were a war veteran,' said Edwin, looking surprised.

'I didn't actually fight in the war. We finished our training when Ian Smith's soldiers surrendered, so I never got the chance to practise all the skills I had learned in Mozambique.'

'So why didn't you join the army after that?' asked Tafara.

'I never really wanted to be a soldier. I went into the army because I was fed up with the segregation and oppression of black people. We needed to bring about black empowerment and take back the lands which had been stolen from us. When the war was over, I decided to venture into something I really had a passion for, which was farming.'

I was happy to hear that we had someone who had the experience of walking such a long distance. His knowledge was going to be vital to our survival.

We took off behind Titus. After what he had told us I knew that, among those in our group, he was the ideal leader. He was also a hunter who seemed to be well versed with most places in our country. In single file we walked behind him, hoping we would not accidentally run into Zanu PF's militia again.

Every single step I took away from Nyamutumbu was painful. The images of Peter, mangled, bloody and unconscious as he was dragged into the school, wouldn't leave my mind. I felt guilt weighing heavily on me. I had to remind myself that I hadn't run away from my husband when he had needed me most. I had done what he wanted me to do - protect our daughter.

I forced the image out of my head, willing any other thought to break through. Like lightning striking, my thought turned towards the rape. I saw the leader of the gang on top of me. I felt him on me again, heard his grunting. I couldn't breathe. I stopped, grabbing my chest. I felt I was about to faint and fell to my knees. Sheila let out a wail.

'Mummy, Mummy! What is wrong?'

I could see the man finishing, a smile of satisfaction on his face as the others cheered. I began shaking uncontrollably. *Oh God, why did you allow this to happen to me? How will I ever forget this? Will it ever be rubbed off from my thoughts? I hate men. All men are dogs.*

My thoughts startled me. If I hated men, how would I feel about Peter if I saw him again? It only took me a moment to know that Peter would always be the exception. He was the only man who would ever make me feel safe.

I saw the figure of a man approach me and swung my arm out in defence, almost punching Brighton, who had come to find out if I was OK. Chiwoniso put her arm on Brighton's shoulder and whispered something in his ear. The others had stopped, watching me as I sobbed angrily. Chiwoniso knelt next to me, wrapping her arms around my shoulders. She didn't say anything. She didn't need to. She had been through exactly what I had been through. She knew what I was seeing.

I took her strength, and after a few minutes, regained my composure. I stood, grasping Sheila's hand, and began walking. The others silently followed.

CHAPTER 5

I was glad that Chiwoniso had brought her daughter, Esther. At least my daughter would have company. The two little girls walked in front of me, holding each other's hands. Although Sheila was younger than Esther, she was slightly taller than her, thanks to the genes she had obviously inherited from my tall husband. The young girls, wearing similar white trainers, marched in front of me like little soldiers. I would often go shopping with Chiwoniso and we would end up buying similar things for our little girls. Sheila had put on a pink cardigan on top of her white dress and Esther was wearing a red dress with a green cardigan top.

Walking behind me was the short and stout Chiwoniso, wearing a blue dress and wrapping herself with a blanket from her waist down. The slim Wellington, our village senior bachelor wearing a white sweater, blue jeans, and a blue golf cap, walked behind us all.

'Wouldn't it have been a good idea if you had left the kids behind?' suggested Wellington.

'We don't know what these barbarians are really up to. They know our relatives and they might go after them in search of us, so it would be very dangerous to leave our kids with any one of our relatives,' replied Chiwoniso.

The other couples' kids were grown up and most of them were in Harare working or pursuing better education, since the schools in rural areas typically offered a poor education.

I looked at the ladies as they clung to their handbags, looking very scared. Then I looked at the men, who were gripping their hunting weapons. Titus and Edwin had each brought two of their dogs. It was funny to observe how different women's and men's priorities were. The women's handbags were full of make-up. I figured my make-up kit wasn't a necessity in the jungle we were travelling through.

In front of the two little girls was Zvanyadza, clutching her husband, Tafara, like a child. She made me think of Peter. I was already missing him. From the moment I had given birth to Sheila, there had not been a single night I had spent without him. Now I found myself in a situation where I didn't know when I was going to see him again. The thought of it felt like someone was cutting my heart with a sharp knife.

He can't be dead! But why did Adamson ask if he was dead? Was he still breathing when they dragged him back to the school? Where is he now? What he is feeling now? Does he know how much I miss him, how much I wish he were here?

My daughter looked back and I winked at her. She smiled, causing my thoughts to drift away from Peter for a while. I smiled back, wondering how she would take the news if her dad were truly dead. She adored him. He was her world. I was glad she didn't know the thoughts that were going through my head.

She was used to seeing her father every day. I remembered the day we went to leave her at her grandparents' place while we went to the couple's retreat. She hugged her dad for more than fifteen minutes and wouldn't let him go. She was crying and grumbling about why kids couldn't go as well. Her grandpa had to pull her away as we left, but she never stopped screaming that she wanted her dad.

We walked for almost half an hour without anyone saying anything. We had to find routes which were as far from homes as possible, since any dogs barking would alert residents and possibly put our lives in serious danger, depending on their political affiliation. In single file we walked in the menacing but beautiful jungles of our country. We were cautious; we would stop occasionally to listen for any voices or human sounds near the routes we were taking. Each time we stopped, we heard only the sounds of our feet sliding through the grass and fallen leaves, wind whistling around tree branches and insects humming in the night.

Esther and Sheila proved stronger than I had ever imagined. We walked about twenty kilometres that night, weaving through the mountains, open fields and caves of Murehwa. The men would take turns carrying the little girls when they complained of tiredness. They seemed to find the whole adventure interesting.

'It's getting brighter now and we need rest. It would be best if we take a break and sleep a bit,' said Titus.

I was so relieved to hear that. My legs were killing me. But each step brought a stab of pain to my sore muscles, which reminded me of the horrible ordeal. Yet the further away we moved from Nyamutumbu, the more my heart ached to be back. It felt as if I was running away from my husband when he needed me most. I would have loved to go back in the morning to find out what had happened to him, but I knew that wasn't an option and that Peter wouldn't want me to. The rape ordeal never stopped flashing in my mind. I wished it was all a dream I would just wake up from.

'I'm hungry Mummy' said Sheila.

'Me too' said Esther.

'And thirsty' retorted Sheila.

'We're all hungry, girls. I'm not sure what we have to give you,' I replied, frustrated.

I was shocked by how easily I was irritated by their request, and how much others' comments began to bother me.

'Here you go, girls,' said Chiwoniso as she took out some bread from her bag.

'You ladies can relax here for now. We'll check to see if there are any streams or wells around' said Titus.

I watched as the two little girls quickly ate the bread they had been given. Giggling and smiling, it looked like they were enjoying the adventure.

I was exhausted. I don't even remember when I fell asleep. But when I woke up, I looked at the time and it was one in the afternoon. I had a headache, but other parts of me ached as well. I shuddered as I moved. The sore muscles were a very real reminder of what those men had done to me, to all the women in our group. I looked around, hoping for a distraction before my thoughts plunged back into the awful memories of that night.

Everyone was fast asleep. Sheila was glued right next to me with Esther next to her. Chiwoniso was on the other side of Esther. It was comforting to have them so close.

I didn't know whether the men had come back or not. If they had returned, they had obviously chosen to sleep far from us. I looked around and could not see any men nearby. I hoped they had brought some water or food, but there was nothing. On my right, not very far from where I was sleeping, was a red-headed green lizard lying on a small rock. It looked at me, nodded its head, and began walking across the rock. It was then I noticed that where the lizard's tail should have been there was just a stub. The lizard had clearly been attacked. And, as all lizards do when attacked, it had defended itself by shedding its tail.

But the lizard's tail would eventually grow back. *Maybe the same thing will happen to Peter,* I thought. *He was attacked and lost his ability to move. But maybe he could walk again. Maybe he could survive.*

I looked away, lifting my face, letting the light and shadows dance across my skin. It was extremely hot, but the trees shielded us from the scorching sun. The forest was nasty and repelling during the night, but disturbingly beautiful during the day.

I closed my eyes, delighting in the sounds of the jungle. The branches creaked in the wind, the birds sang, creating peaceful, calm music, and the lizards scrambled up the trees. I smiled. In that moment, it was hard to imagine we had all just been through Hell.

The sound of snoring broke me out of my meditation. Gertrude had her mouth wide open and a handful of flies hovered over her face, obviously enjoying the stinking smell that emitted from her unwashed mouth. I chuckled while trying to get up, but I was more tired and hungry than I had realized. I had no energy at all. I wondered how many more days we were going to continue like this, on empty stomachs. I feared our escape would prove to be one of the most difficult tasks I had to go through in my life.

I wondered where I was going to get the energy and strength for the next move. I began to think of the last physical trial I had endured - giving birth to Sheila. At least then I had known that with one big, strong push the baby would come out. But with this ordeal, no one knew where it would go or how it would end. I was tired and felt I had had enough with just a day's walk. Thinking about doing this for even one week was overwhelming, and the fact that no one knew how long it would take to walk to South Africa made it even worse.

I looked at the two beautiful, innocent girls sleeping peacefully, unaware of the mammoth task which lay ahead of them. I sat there quietly, thinking about the events of the previous night. How quickly things had changed for me and my family. I wished it had been a terrible dream, that I would wake up and be back home with Peter and Sheila. But this was reality. My thoughts continued to drift back to Peter. I longed to go back, to see if he survived. But I wasn't sure how to navigate my way through the jungle. *Where is my husband right now? Did he get to safety? Who is nursing his wounds?* My thoughts were interrupted by the waking up of Gertrude.

'Morning,' she said, yawning.

'Morning? Does it look like morning to you?' I asked, smiling back at her.

'Sorry. What time is it now?'

I looked at my watch. I was surprised to see that I had spent almost thirty minutes just sitting and staring at the ladies sleeping around me. I couldn't recall the last time I had simply woken up lost in thought. I was used to running around every time I woke up. I normally woke up at five in the morning to begin my morning chores, which often included sweeping outside our compound and making sure breakfast was ready before my husband woke up. It was shocking to think how life had just changed for me. I never imagined I would be in a situation in which I didn't know whether my husband was dead or alive, or in which I didn't know the next time I would be able to eat.

'It's one-thirty,' I said as I looked at my daughter, who had just turned around.

'It's that late already?' Gertrude mumbled.

'Aargh!'

We all jumped, either waking from our sleep or turning around to look at Ruramai, who had just woken up screaming.

She sat up and looked like she was about to run, so I jumped and grabbed her. With her eyes wide open, she looked at me like she had never seen me before. I struggled as she tried to break free. She was slimmer than me, allowing me to hold her down easily.

'Ruramai! Ruramai!' I exclaimed, shaking her to try and wake her up.

'Oh, it's just you,' she said, but her brown, squinty eyes were still wide open, revealing how frightened she was.

'Bad dream, was it?' asked Gertrude.

'Where is Edwin?' she asked, looking for her husband.

I frowned slightly. *At least she has someone's shoulder to cry on during this difficult journey. I wish Peter was here as well.* I took the knitted hat which had fallen from her head, revealing her curly grey hair, and helped her put it back on. She was only 41 but had grey hair; a condition she said was hereditary, as most of her family members turned grey prematurely. We had got to know each other at the couples' retreat, where she had told me all about her family. She had met Edwin 25 years ago, dated for three years, then married and had two boys and a girl. The boys were 20 and 21, the girl was 18. Their children had done very well and were in Harare studying at the university.

'What's going on?' asked Zvanyadza, who was woken up by Ruramai's screams.

'Everything is OK. She just had a nightmare,' replied Gertrude.

'Oh, I see,' said Zvanyadza as she sat up.

We sat there for a while chatting but I could see everyone was hungry. I looked around, hoping that we would see the men coming with plenty of food in their hands.

CHAPTER 6

I looked at Ruramai as we continued chatting. I wondered if her nightmares were similar to the ones I had had. Though I hadn't woken up screaming, I had been terrified. I had slept fitfully as the rape played through my dreams over and over. Ruramai was sweating, clearly frightened by what she had dreamed. As she tried to engage herself in our conversation, I could see that she was still shaken by her dream. I figured all of the women in our group must have been put through the same rape ordeal, but no one seemed to want to discuss it. No one was able to go back to sleep, so we started discussing the mammoth task ahead of us.

'How many more days are we going to go on like this?' I asked as the reality set in of how difficult this was going to be.

'Let's not get discouraged on the first day, ladies. Let's just keep walking and pray that God will provide another mode of transportation,' replied Zvanyadza.

'I'm not discouraged necessarily, but I think Nyasha has a point,' said Happiness. 'This is going to be a rather difficult task, we need to talk about how to accomplish it.'

'No one here has ever been to South Africa before, so how can we plan to get there?' pondered Chiwoniso.

Zvanyadza chuckled. 'And since when did we women start

planning these things? Isn't that the role of the man?'

Happiness furrowed her brow, clearly concerned. 'But there is nothing wrong in helping our men with the planning. Our contributions could be of much help to them.'

Zvanyadza began debating on the proper role of us women in helping us survive. Others began joining in as well. The argument was getting heated, as some wanted us to leave the planning to the men and some felt it was everyone's responsibility to contribute to finding a place of refuge for us.

'*Tisvikewo?* [May we approach]?' shouted a male voice, interrupting the argument.

'*Svikai zvenyu* [You are welcome here],' replied Zvanyadza, who had recognized the husky voice of her husband, Tafara.

The men were now up and looked ready to go on with the journey. But I needed food first; I was starving.

'*Marara sei?* [Did you have a good night's sleep]?' asked Brighton.

'*Tarara kana mararawo* [We have slept well, we hope you all slept well],' we replied in harmony, like a choir.

'Are you ladies arguing or gossiping about something?' asked Tafara, smiling.

'Well, since we don't have a plan, we were trying to create one, that's all,' said Ruramai.

'Well, for now, here is the plan. We will walk in the evenings and rest during daytime. We have to stay as far from the houses as possible. If we keep the same pace we did last night, we should reach Marondera in two days' time,' said Titus.

'Why Marondera? Isn't that drifting away from the route we should be taking?' asked Zvanyadza.

'Marondera still has a vast number of wild animals, which means we can do a little bit of hunting before we proceed. Let's not forget we'll need food to have the energy to get us to South Africa,' replied Titus.

'Food is what we need right now,' said Ruramai.

'We know and we are working towards that,' said Titus.

'There is a stream behind those rocks on your left. You can take a bath there if you wish. We are going to try to find you something to eat,' said Edwin.

Although food was of more importance to me at the moment, a bath sounded like the next best thing. I felt very dirty after what had happened to me the previous night. I needed to feel clean again. I just hoped, as I washed away the dirt on me, the memory of it all and the pain would somehow be washed away as well.

All the women seemed anxious to clean themselves. We watched the men leave with their hunting tools and four dogs leading the way. I prayed for God to be merciful in helping them find food for us.

We picked up our belongings and headed towards the stream. The water was clean and warm, which was perfect. We bathed the little girls first and then we bathed as they played close by. We could overhear their game.

'I will be the mother and you will be my daughter,' said Sheila.

'No. I don't want to be your daughter. I will be your husband,' said Esther.

This is the same game we used to play when we were little kids, I thought. *We used to imitate everything that we saw our parents do.*

'Fine then, you will be the husband,' said Sheila, somewhat dejected.

We watched quietly, entertained in waiting to see how well they were going to play the self-imposed new roles they had given each other. We all smiled as Esther tried to imitate the way her father walked. Sheila moved a little bit further away from Esther and sat down the way she used to see me sitting when I cooked food.

'They remind me of us,' whispered Chiwoniso.

She was right. It made me smile to think that our two daughters were playing the same games we used to. I didn't want to alert the girls that we were watching them, so I just silently nodded my head in agreement. Chiwoniso and I had grown up together. We were neighbours in Kasino village, which was about twenty kilometres north of Nyamutumbu village. We had grown up together, went to the same school, and have remained best friends through everything.

I had actually met Peter through Brighton, Chiwoniso's husband. I still vividly remember Chiwoniso's excitement when she had first told me about Brighton after she had first met him. It was at Musami Hospital, which happened to be about halfway between Nyamutumbu village and Kasino village. She had taken her mother for a medical checkup and Brighton had escorted his mother to the hospital for malaria treatment on the same day. It was on a Wednesday and the following Saturday Brighton walked almost twenty kilometres to see her. That madness continued for almost six months, resulting in Chiwoniso becoming pregnant. Her mum was furious, not only because she had become pregnant before getting married, but because the father of her unborn child was someone who wasn't from our village and someone they knew nothing about. Parents preferred their children to be married in the same village with families they knew and respected.

Brighton had proved his love for Chiwoniso by arranging a traditional wedding. He came with his friends and relatives to pay *lobola* (bride's money). Peter came along as well, never taking his eyes off of me during the whole marriage ceremony. After the ceremony, Brighton took his new wife to his home in Nyamutumbu.

It was a week later, when Chiwoniso had visited her parents, that she told me there was a guy in Nyamutumbu village who had a crush on me and was always talking about me. I was pretty sure I knew who it was, but I pretended I didn't.

She arranged a meeting and Peter didn't waste any time. He poured his heart out to me, telling me how he felt. Since there was no one I was going out with, I didn't refuse and we started going out. Our relationship was not all moonlight and roses, however, as it was received with fierce resistance from my family.

Peter was from a poor family and had failed to complete his secondary education because of lack of funds. To them, he had nothing to offer. They wanted someone who would pay a lot of money and cattle for me as *lobola*. While I was dating Peter, they were grooming me to be married to James, the son of a rich businessman in our village. Discussions had taken place between my father, who was a Muslim, and James's father, who was also a Muslim. They were both pleased with the arrangement. My mother, being Catholic, was not terribly supportive of an arranged marriage. She preferred James as her future son-in-law because of his family's status in the village, but I didn't want to sacrifice my happiness in order to please my parents. And Peter made me happier than anyone else had. As it was my life, I felt I was the one who should have the final say about who was going to be my husband.

James was a well-known 'player'. He was arrogant and proud. He was known for dumping girls and saying they were ugly after he had slept with them. Because of his family's money and status most girls had fallen for him, only to be hurt in the end. He had tried to get into my pants many times as well, but I wasn't easily swept away by material things. I wanted to give myself to my true love and wanted someone who would feel the same.

Peter was totally different from James. He was genuine, loving, kind, and serious about settling down. Peter was my obvious choice. I had fallen deeply in love with him. I was prepared to die for him and I didn't care what people said. We tried to keep our affair a secret, but within a short period of time everyone in the village knew and the news reached my parents. My parents told me they were never going to accept Peter into our family and told me to end the relationship, but I stood my ground. I told them Peter was my choice and there was nothing they could do to make me change my mind. Everyone in my village said I was either under an evil spell or stupid to want a poor man instead of one from a wealthy family. Only Chiwoniso had stood by me.

I endured my family's disapproval for three months. When the pressure escalated into abuse, I decided to run away. At one time my brothers began beating up Peter when he came to see me and told him he should never set his foot in our village again. The only way we could see each was for me to visit him. When my parents found out I was going to Nyamutumbu to see him, the beatings came to me.

I had had enough. I couldn't handle that kind of abuse anymore. Peter's parents knew what was going on and accepted me with open arms. They talked to the chief in Nyamutumbu and we were given a piece of land to build our home. Peter and I started living together as husband and wife, against my parents' wishes. Chiwoniso was pleased that I had moved closer to her and our friendship continued to grow. To me, she was more like a sister.

After a few weeks I started to see some changes in my body. I knew what that meant and gave Peter the news. He was thrilled. Once my parents learned I was pregnant, they saw that it was too late to make us break up, so they didn't oppose Peter when he offered to pay *lobola*. He was ordered to pay a cow as punishment for eloping with me. He couldn't pay all they demanded, though, and he still owed them some money and cattle. But the most important thing was that they accepted him as their son-in-law. *Oh Peter,* I thought mournfully. *I pray to God you're all right.*

'Darling, dinner is ready,' said Sheila as she moulded some wet mud together.

'I told you I want it with meat and you are giving me okra. What is wrong with you, woman?' shouted Esther, making us all burst into laughter.

The two girls jumped when they heard us laugh, abandoning their game. They became shy when they realized we were watching them.

'Is this how your husband treats you, Chiwoniso?' asked Zvanyadza.

'My husband does not talk to me like that, if he knows what is good for him,' replied Chiwoniso

'So where did your daughter hear that from?' asked Ruramai.

'I don't know. She must have made it up,' replied Chiwoniso, smiling.

We wished we had not distracted them. I was eager to hear how Sheila was going to respond. My thoughts drifted to the many times I had told Peter that dinner was ready. I had not realized how much he meant to me. I felt hollow inside without him. I missed him so much. *Will I ever get that opportunity again to prepare dinner for Peter? Is he alive? If he is alive does he want a raped woman as his wife?* I thought. We then continued with our bath, trying to listen as the little girls tried to figure out a new game to play.

CHAPTER 7

After finishing bathing we went back to wait for the men, hoping they would return soon with food. I felt fresh, but the memories of the previous night had not washed away. I could see from their faces that the other women had not forgotten it either. Ruramai had tried to hide her underwear from our view; it had a fair amount of blood on it. As Gertrude had stepped into the pond, I had noticed dried blood on her legs too. We had all been through a horrible ordeal. It was something that would leave permanent scars. And yet, even with those awful memories constantly invading my thoughts, I never stopped thinking about my husband's fate.

The Most High God had smiled on the men, as they had had a good day. They had managed to catch a rabbit and a few birds. They also brought some wild fruits and had stolen some maize. Stealing wasn't the best thing to do, as we were trying to keep a low profile, but we obviously needed to do whatever we could to survive the long journey.

We started a fire, which was easy, thanks to the chain-smoking Wellington, and roasted the maize and meat. We ate everything like hungry pigs, leaving only a few fruits to eat while walking. We relaxed, waiting for it to get dark, as we only walked in the evenings. I was trying not to think of Peter, but the couples in our group made me think of him. Especially Titus and Happiness, who were always glued to each other, making me wish Peter was around. I had never seen a couple so in love at their age.

Where is Peter now? How is he feeling? Who is nursing his wounds? Will he still want me once he truly comes to terms with me being raped?

'Come on guys, let's get moving,' said Titus as the sun was setting. I paused, looking at the brilliant red grazing the tops of the bright green trees. While I hated travelling through the jungle, I was surprised to find myself spending just a moment enjoying the beauty of my country.

We picked up our belongings and walked behind our leader. Titus proved to be well versed in all the skills we needed to survive in the dangerous but beautiful jungles of Zimbabwe. Next to him was Happiness, clutching onto him with eyes full of love. This old couple amazed us all. Their love seemed so new, like two teenagers who had just fallen in love. They were always by each other's side.

They were both in their late fifties, but they were still not fed up with each other. I remembered how, in the morning, Happiness had protested and complained about sleeping away from her husband. At their age, I wondered if they were still showing their love to each other physically. It was good to see their love still burning. I hoped it would be the same between me and Peter, if he were still alive and if he still wanted a now dirty, damaged woman like me. It was hard for me to think that way, but that was the reality. If I was being honest with myself, I knew there was a high probability that I might never see my husband again.

The rest of us followed behind them. I felt refreshed as the food had given me renewed energy. I wanted us to get to our next resting place as quickly as possible.

'Can you please wait for me, I want to relieve myself,' said Chiwoniso, who was behind me.

I had almost forgotten how often my best friend had to go to the bathroom. I remembered the day she came to my home, crying after she had been told by the doctor that she was diabetic. She thought she was going to die within a short period of time. We walked over to the village shops together and she was relieved after getting more of an explanation from our village nurse, who explained to her what kind of a disease it was and how she could control it. One side-effect, however, was the more frequent urge she had to go to the bathroom. We stopped to allow her to relieve herself.

'OK, hurry up madam!' shouted Titus.

As a mark of respect, all the men continued to walk and stopped slightly further away from us. Chiwoniso dashed aside and went behind a small bush.

We patiently waited for her, conversing among each other. We respected Chiwoniso and didn't want her to feel self-conscious about her condition. We tried to have upbeat conversations to make sure she knew we didn't mind the frequent stopping.

'*Amaihwe kani* [Oh my mum]! *Tenzi wangu kani* [Oh my Lord]! *Mwari wangu kani* [Oh my God]!' she came back screaming, holding her leg.

Scared, reacting to her screams, we all yelled for the men and ran towards them. We hadn't asked what had happened to her or what she had just seen. We were all reacting out of fear.

'What is it? What is it!' asked some of the men as they all ran towards us.

'*Pane chandiruma kani* [Something has bitten me]! *Pane chandiruma kani*[Something has bitten me]!' cried out Chiwoniso.

'What has bitten you, darling? What is it?' asked her worried husband.

'I don't know! I don't know what it is *baba* Esther! Oh God, help me!' my best friend sobbed.

I took the sobbing Esther into my arms as they attended to Chiwoniso. She was sweating and looked very scared. I could see that she was in serious pain.

'Let me see where the bite is' said Titus. She sat down as Titus and her husband examined her.

'It looks like she has been bitten by a snake,' said Titus. 'Give me your belt. Let's tie this around her thigh so that the poison will not spread to the rest of her body.'

This was the last thing I wanted to hear Titus say. I hoped it wasn't a poisonous snake that had bitten her. I didn't want to lose my best friend, not in that way. The mere mention of a snake made her cry more. We all knew what this could mean. I could see the worry on her and her husband's face.

'It's important that we know what kind of a snake it is,' said Tafara. 'That will help us to know the kind of treatment she requires and will help decide on the course of action.'

He was right. We could easily assume it was a snake while it could have been a small insect or a scorpion. It was important we knew exactly what had bitten her.

We stood and watched as they tied a tourniquet around her leg. The other men went to where she had been bitten and lit up the grass with a torch. It didn't take long to see what had bitten her, as the snake tried to flee from the burning grass. She had been bitten by a *Bitis atropos*, a species of viper, which was almost fifty centimeters long. They pounced on it and killed it instantly.

'This snake is venomous. We have to rush her to the hospital,' said Wellington.

'We are in the middle of nowhere. Where are we going to find a hospital?' asked Zvanyadza.

She had a point. We all looked at each other, not knowing what to do. I inwardly prayed for the worst not to happen. My best friend was crying and sweating, the poison clearly spreading fast. I wished I had some sort of power to draw the poison out of her. I might have lost my husband, but I didn't want to lose my best friend as well. But sitting around wasn't going to help in any way; we needed to get going.

'Let's get moving and pray that we'll come across a clinic as soon as possible,' said Titus, as though reading my thoughts.

'Come on, jump on my back' said Brighton to his wife. We helped her get up onto Brighton's back. We left, but we were not moving as fast as we had been the night before. We had to stop often to allow Brighton to rest, as it wasn't appropriate for any other man to carry her on his back and no other woman had the power or energy to relieve Brighton. I wished I could help, but Chiwoniso was heavier than I.

She was getting weaker and weaker every kilometre we walked. She desperately needed medical help. Using a piece of the wrap she had brought with her, we fastened her on to her husband's back. Walking very close to Brighton, I kept massaging her back, hoping to comfort her.

After walking a few kilometres, I looked at my best friend and didn't like what I saw. White foam was coming out of the corners of her mouth and her head was flopping around with each step Brighton took. From what I could tell, she didn't appear to be breathing properly.

'Wellington, please come and take a closer look at Chiwoniso, she seems to be getting worse,' I whispered to Wellington, who was walking behind me.

'Let's take another rest, guys!' Wellington shouted to the group ahead of us.

They stopped and we looked for a place to sit down. Seeing how my best friend looked, I decided to take the small girls away as they examined her.

As we walked into the jungle, we heard only silence, and then a terrible cry from Brighton.

'Oh God why! Why *amai vaEsthe*r! Why! *Wadireiko kudaro mukadzi wangu* [Why have you decided to do this to me my wife]! *Wandirwadzisa amai vemwana* [You have caused me unbearable pain, mother of my child]!' Brighton was sobbing uncontrollably.

I stopped walking and began to feel dizzy. I sat on a fallen tree stump, trying to focus my vision. The girls were standing next to me, staring at me curiously. I didn't want to accept that my best friend was gone. She had always been my supporter, my champion when things were rough. I didn't know what to do. I felt my face flush, blood rushing to my head, my heart beating loudly in my ears. A horrible feeling was rising in me. My stomach felt as if it had a knot in it. The pain was different but deep. I felt as if my chest had been smashed by a hammer. I couldn't breathe. I couldn't believe I would never see my best friend again. I had never seen it coming, even when we were attacked by Mugabe's gang. I always thought she would be there for me.

Esther's cries snapped me out of my internal mourning. She was straining her neck, trying to see her mother and father, but was fearful to leave Sheila and me.

'What has happened to my mum? Oh, my mum! I want my mum!' Esther cried. She sprinted away, joining in her father's sobbing as she tried to go where her mother lay dead.

Sheila and I quickly followed her, standing at her side as she looked at her mother. I gripped her hand tightly. The other women were attempting to pull her away. It wasn't good for a child to see a corpse, especially that of her mother. She could have nightmares all her life, seeing such a tragic thing. But Esther would not move away from her mother. I tried to stay strong, but the tears overwhelmed me and I started crying as well. Brighton and Esther's grief touched us all. I eventually looked up and noticed everyone crying, including all the men. But I was grieving for more. Because I had chosen to save my daughter, I didn't know if Peter was alive or dead. I had made a choice, and I had to live with that choice. Peter might have followed the same path as Chiwoniso.

We all sat down, grieving for our friend. I wasn't sure how much time had passed. To think she had survived being raped and had escaped from what likely would have been a death sentence, only to die from a snake bite in the forest. It was a sobering thought.

Now the biggest challenge was what we were going to do with her body. Our culture did not allow burying someone without notifying her blood relatives, but we were very far from them.

Edwin, Tafara and Wellington had stepped to the side of the group, discussing what was to be done.

'We should go and bury her near the river. It's easier to dig there, considering we don't have any digging tools,' said Edwin.

Wellington nodded. 'With all of us helping, it should go fairly quickly.'

Brighton, overhearing what they were saying, jumped up from his wife's side. 'No, I'm not dumping my wife in this jungle. This is my decision.'

No one disputed what he said. She was his wife and it was up to him to decide how he wanted her to be buried. In our culture, the relatives of the deceased determine how they should be buried. To make matters even more complicated, we had to consider exactly where she would be buried. Her relatives would eventually be notified, and they would want to both see her body and bring her remains back to their village, as was tradition. Finding a place that was both accessible and memorable would be difficult.

'Put her on my back, she is coming with us. I'm not leaving my wife here,' said Brighton as he knelt down, getting ready to carry her on her back again.

We all looked at each other, apprehension written on our faces. Brighton's request was pure madness, but I couldn't tell him that. No one could. But at the same time, no one could blame him. We knew how in love they were. With Esther, they were a family and part of that family was now gone. Anyone in Brighton's situation would have been ripped into pieces by what had just happened.

The men did as he wished. Titus and Wellington pulled Chiwoniso up and laid her on his back. They secured her there, using her wrap as they had before. Brighton got up and started walking. Gertrude picked up the sobbing Esther and followed behind, not letting her look at her mother's dead body bouncing on Brighton's back. We walked very slowly behind them, as most of us were still in shock. We never stopped crying. Chiwoniso's sudden departure had pained us greatly.

We had walked a few more kilometres when Brighton fell down in exhaustion, sobbing and wailing. It seemed to have dawned on him that not only was his wife no more, but he couldn't keep Chiwoniso with him. He had to start living without her.

He unfastened the wrap and gently lowered her to the ground. Then he took Esther into his arms and walked a short distance away, settling under a large *muhacha* tree. The two sobbed together for a while. It was heartbreaking to see the pain they were going through.

After some time, Titus walked up to Brighton, placing a hand gently on his shoulder.

'We are going to find a place where we can bury her' he said.

This time Brighton didn't argue. He nodded his head in agreement. The men left in search of a place to bury Chiwoniso. While they were gone, the rest of us gathered around her, preparing her body to be buried. We fixed her hair and adjusted her clothes. Tears started flowing down my face when I looked at her. It looked as if she was sleeping and would wake up at any moment.

The men came back and took her body with them. After an hour they returned, looking exhausted by the work they had done. Tafara told Brighton they found a beautiful place by a stream. He assured Brighton it would be very easy to locate if anyone ever came back.

That night, my best friend was laid to rest. I couldn't believe I was never going to see her again. I thought of all the good times we had shared. I remembered how she had made life easy for me in Nyamutumbu and how she had stood by me, and I by her, through everything. She was not just a friend. She was more like a sister to me. I recalled the time I had visited her and she had told me if anything were to happen to her, she would want me to look after her daughter.

'Stepmothers are very cruel, Nyasha. I wouldn't want a woman I didn't know looking after my daughter. In case I die, Nyasha, I want you to look after Esther,' she had told me.

I walked over with Sheila to her grave and stood, looking at the spot, pretending I could see Chiwoniso.

'I promise to look after Esther. Rest in peace, my friend, my Chiwoniso. Till we meet again,' I tearfully said as I dropped some sand on her grave.

As a way to render our respect to our friend, and to allow Brighton and Esther to mourn the loss of a wife and mother, Titus called off walking that night. We sat at her grave singing and crying, eventually falling asleep until the next morning.

CHAPTER 8

We relaxed the next day, waiting until it began getting dark before we took off again and continued on our journey. In three days, we had reached Marondera and were glad that we were making progress. At least we were far from the people who knew that we were members of the opposition party.

Marondera was not too different from Murehwa. Much of the farmland was uncultivated. The land was lush with *miombo* (Brachystegia) trees. Rock flora covered much of the landscape, with some areas filled with seasonal ponds and grasslands. With abundant vegetation and streams running throughout the land, it was no wonder antelopes and wild pigs flocked there.

I began to think that maybe God was with us. On our first night in Marondera, the men went hunting and came back with a wild pig. We feasted and had enough meat to last us more than a week. I never understood why Titus wanted us to come through Marondera, but now I understood. It had a large population of wild animals. He must have come here hunting himself. We were grateful that the men had been wise in deciding to bring their dogs along with us as well, as they had been instrumental in catching the wild pig.

We continued as previously planned, walking at night and

resting during the day. In eight days we had covered about 160 kilometres, eventually leaving behind Marondera and journeying through Gutu. I was very tired, as we all were, but was happy we were making progress.

The sudden death of Chiwoniso had affected us greatly. The day she died was still fresh in my mind—it felt as if it had just happened. I missed her greatly. But what Brighton and Esther went through was worse. Many times, Esther would wake up asking for her mother. Once she remembered what happened, she would start crying. My heart broke when I heard her, and while the others were trying to comfort Esther they would try to comfort me as well. Sheila was very concerned for her friend. I was proud of how my little daughter worked hard to try and console her best friend, always holding her hand and making sure she slept next to her when we stopped for the day.

Brighton had lost his appetite for almost three days, at first refusing to eat anything after Chiwoniso's death. The men worked very hard to try and pull him out of his depression. Titus showed his leadership qualities as he took Brighton on walks, counselling him as best he could. We were all still scared, knowing that what had happened to Chiwoniso could happen to any of us. But we had no choice, we had to keep going. Zimbabwe was no longer safe for us and anyone who opposed Mugabe was no longer welcome. Our quest for freedom was now taking us into places we never imagined we would go.

'Mum, why do people die?' asked Sheila, my inquisitive little girl.

'It is how life is, my dear. Everyone will die at their own

time and go to be with Jesus. Then one day, God will have us all meet again,' I replied, praying that she wouldn't drag out the conversation any longer.

Esther, who had been holding Sheila's hand, looking down at the ground as she walked, looked up at me.

'So is my mum with Jesus now?' she asked, her eyes reflecting deep sadness.

I was silent, feeling sad as I tried to respond. Aside from feeling grief for Chiwoniso, I couldn't help but wonder if Peter was with her.

'Yes, and she must be looking at us right now,' replied Gertrude after she had noticed that I wasn't comfortable talking about Chiwoniso's death.

'I miss her. I wish I could be with her and Jesus,' said Esther.

I was surprised hearing such comments from a little girl of her age. She clearly didn't realise what she was saying. Dying in order to be with her mother was a depressing thought. But every child needs a mother and I just hoped that I would be able to fill that role for her.

'It is God who decides who he should take. When you have grown up and at God's chosen time you will go and be with your mother,' said Gertrude as she took her into her arms.

'But why does God have to take us? Why doesn't he just leave us here with our families?' asked Sheila.

'God loves us dearly, but He knows what is best for us. The place He takes us is very beautiful and better than this place, but only good people will go there,' I replied, helping Gertrude.

Esther and Sheila were both silent, thinking over what we had said.

'Girls, let me tell you a lovely African fairy tale,' said Ruramai, trying to lighten the mood and steer the discussion away from death.

'Yes! Yes!' screamed Sheila with excitement. She loved being told stories. I always told her animal fairy tales every evening before she went to bed. Peter would try and chip in here and there, but I was the expert storyteller.

'Come and sit next to me if you want to hear this exciting fairy tale,' said Ruramai as she sat down.

Sheila jumped up and sat close to her, eagerly waiting to hear the story from Ruramai. Esther dragged her feet. She looked as if she wasn't that excited about hearing the fairy tale. Hopefully, she would listen to the story and forget for a moment the pain she felt upon losing her mother.

'Once upon a time in Mutoko... ' Ruramai began. She paused and looked at the girls, waiting for them to respond.

'Once upon a time in Mutoko' said Ruramai again.

They stared at her, waiting for her to continue the story.

'You girls have to respond by saying, 'Speak, Auntie Ruramai!' every time,' said Happiness.

'Speak, Auntie Ruramai!' said the young girls simultaneously.

'Good girls,' said Happiness.

'There once was a very clever rabbit called Tsuro Magen'a and a foolish baboon called Chihombori,' said Ruramai.

'Speak, Auntie Ruramai!' we all shouted, assisting the girls in responding.

'Both animals were madly in love with a very beautiful girl who was called Tanaka. They were competing to win her heart,' said Ruramai.

'Speak, Auntie Ruramai!' we all responded.

'They both decided to cook her some food. The food she loved the most would determine which animal would go out with her,' said Ruramai.

'Speak, Auntie Ruramai!'

'Time to get back on the road now guys!' shouted Titus as he stood up.

'Oh, it's not fair! Can we just finish this fairy tale please?' cried out Sheila. They were now very eager to know how the fairy tale ended and who among the two animals had won Tanaka's heart. Even Esther had brightened up. She was very interested in the story. I wished we had enough time to tell them the tale.

'Don't worry girls, I will find another time to finish the story for you,' said Ruramai as she stroked their hair.

We took off again, forcing our blistered feet and tired legs to walk another twenty kilometres that night. We were now like one family; we were getting closer and closer each day as we got to know each other more.

Many people in our group were starting to open up about some dark secrets in their lives. The person I was most interested to know about was Gertrude, a widow who had endured the pain of being painted as a witch throughout the village. She was tall and slim, making me wonder if the things she had had to put up with daily had made her lose so much weight.

All I knew was that she had been married in Mutare and had been brought back to the village after the death of her husband. Her late husband's family had accused her of killing him. Her late husband's relatives had even refused to pass her on to his brothers, which was the normal Shona custom.

They said they wanted her to be cleansed of witchcraft first before she could come back. Rumours had circulated in the village that she had inherited witchcraft powers from her mother. But she had kept tight-lipped about it all and never tried to defend herself. Wearing a black dress, as all widows are required to do, she walked beside me.

'I'm very sorry about everything you have gone through with Peter and Chiwoniso. I know exactly how it feels to lose someone very close to you,' said Gertrude as she put her hand on my shoulder.

'Thanks. If it were not for everyone's support and comfort, I don't know how I would have coped. It's a blessing to have you guys around,' I said.

'When my husband died, instead of receiving comfort, all I got was torture and abuse,' said Gertrude. 'I don't wish for any female to go through what I went through.'

I could feel pain and regret in her voice when she mentioned her husband. I felt it was a good opportunity to hear the real story of exactly what had happened to him.

'I'm so sorry to hear that. I hope you don't mind me asking, but how exactly did your husband die?'

I was surprised by the sudden change in everyone's faces around us. It was obvious to them that I had asked something they believed wasn't supposed to be asked. I couldn't blame them, as they too had heard the rumours that had circulated about Gertrude's life. But I preferred to hear it from the horse's mouth.

'I had been married to Kelvin for ten years' she said. 'We had worked very hard and had progressed from having nothing to being proud owners of a few shops in Mutare. The weekend that he died, we had gone to Mutasa village, which is a few kilometres from Mutare. We had gone there for a family function. Everything went well and we had a good time. All his brothers and sisters were at the function, which we had financed, buying all of the food and alcohol for them.

'On Sunday afternoon, Kelvin insisted that we had to go home. I refused to go, as I had seen him drinking too much that day and felt he wasn't fit to drive. We got into a heated argument, but I stood my ground. I even went as far as hiding the car keys from him. His older brother became furious, telling my husband that he wasn't a man as he always allowed me to control everything.

'His brother accused me of using love potions to make his brother stupid and not think properly so that I and my relatives could enjoy all the proceeds from the business we were running. He even lied that a witch doctor had told him I was planning to kill my husband so that I would have all the business and assets to myself.

'I couldn't take the insults and lies any more. They were too much, so I decided to leave. I gave my husband the car keys and went to look for a taxi. My husband got into his car and found me still on the road waiting for a taxi. He persuaded me to get in the car and we left.'

'My husband was still drunk. He was speeding and, after a few kilometres, he lost control and we crashed. We were both seriously injured and were rushed to Mutare General Hospital. The hospital demanded upfront fees before any treatment could be carried out, so all our relatives were notified and, luckily, my brother had included me on his medical aid plan, so they started treating me. Money for my husband's treatment was given to his older brother to bring to the hospital, but for some reason, a thirty-minute journey took him two hours.

'By the time he arrived, my husband had bled to death. His excuse was that his car had broken down and that some evil spirits, which I had supposedly sent, made him lose his way. My husband's older brother brought a witch doctor to the funeral to strength his case. The rest of the relatives believed his version of the story and I was accused of killing my husband. Our fight before the accident worked against me. After the funeral, I was humiliated and kicked out of my home. I lost everything my husband and I had worked so hard for and today that brother of my late husband is the proud owner of our shops. I know who killed my husband and one day the truth will set me free,' concluded Gertrude.

'Eish! Your brother-in-law is very wicked,' said Happiness.

'My dear, you have to forgive me for believing the village rumours,' Ruramai said.

'Didn't you have any children with your husband?' inquired Zvanyadza.

'I have three boys. Tinashe is nine years old, Tadiwa is seven and Shelton is five. They said the kids were theirs and would not be going anywhere,' replied Gertrude.

'You have to sue them. Don't allow them to get away with that,' I said passionately.

'I'm in the process of doing that, but my brother-in-law is always bribing the officials so they keep postponing the court date.'

'In this country, as long as you belong to Zanu PF or have some money, you can do anything and get away with it,' said Zvanyadza.

We continued walking in silence for a while. It seemed the mention of Zanu PF by Zvanyadza had brought some sad memories to every one of us. We were now all scared to mention the ruling party.

CHAPTER 9

As we were walking down a dusty road somewhere around a village in Gutu, Tafara looked back. 'Someone's coming!' he exclaimed.

We all looked behind us and saw the lights of an approaching car coming up the road, interrupting our conversation. We were a bit worried, as we didn't know who was in the car. It could have been the police or soldiers, for all we knew.

'Don't worry, keep walking!' shouted Titus.

We kept walking, but the frequent glances behind our path clearly showed how worried everyone was. When the car passed us we realised it was a lorry. The driver slowly drove past us and stopped some distance ahead.

'Don't worry about him, just keep walking!' shouted Titus again.

We eventually got to where the driver had stopped and Titus moved to the driver's side of the lorry to talk to the driver.

'This is a dangerous area to be walking in at this time of the night with children,' said the driver. 'Where are you going?'

'We are on our way to South Africa,' said Titus.

'South Africa!' laughed the driver. 'Do you know what kind

of a journey that is, especially at night? Why didn't you wait until morning?'

'It's an emergency. Our lives are in danger and we are on the run,' replied Titus.

'How many are you?' asked the driver.

'Ten adults and two children.'

'I am going to Lutumba. It's about twenty-two kilometres from Beitbridge. I can drop you off there,' said the driver.

'That is very kind, but we don't have any money to give you,' said Titus.

'Who is talking about money here? Jump in and let's go before I change my mind,' said the driver as he revved his lorry.

Titus hurried back to the group.

'Everyone, this generous gentleman is going to help us!' shouted Titus. 'Climb into the back of the lorry; he will drive us close to Beitbridge.'

'The wind back there can be terrible' shouted the river. 'Let the kids come and sit with me here in front.'

'Nyasha, go sit with the girls in front; the rest of us will jump in the back,' said Titus.

I climbed in front with the girls and watched as the other ladies struggled to jump into the back of the lorry. Everyone eventually jumped in except Happiness, who couldn't find the strength to lift her body up into the lorry. The driver impatiently revved his engine as he waited for Happiness to jump in.

'Give me your hand,' said Titus as he tried to help his wife.

Happiness looked at him nervously, either worried he couldn't help her or embarrassed that he had to help her.

'There is space for one more person up here,' shouted the driver. Happiness looked very relieved. She came and joined me in the front seat.

'Thank you' said Happiness as she sat next to me.

'You are welcome' said the driver as he put the lorry into gear.

'*Mafotofoto* [obese],' I teased her.

'Mind your tongue, little girl, otherwise you will have no teeth by the time you get to my age,' said Happiness, smiling.

The girls sat on our laps and we watched the driver as he struggled with the stiff steering wheel.

'Mind my cabbages back there!' shouted the driver as he started driving. 'There are some oranges back there as well. You can help yourselves.'

'Thank you!' Edwin shouted back.

We were the lucky ones, though, because there was a lot of food in the front. We had biscuits, bananas, apples, and oranges. The driver was truly an angel sent from heaven to help us. I have never met such a generous man in my whole life.

'You have to thank God for these two little girls. If it weren't for them, I wouldn't have stopped,' said the driver.

'Why is that?' asked Happiness.

'There are a lot of criminals in this area and they use all kinds of tricks to get the drivers to stop, but when I saw these girls, I knew something must be wrong.'

'We want you to know that we really appreciate all you have done for us. We pray that God will richly bless you,' I said.

'Amen! You are welcome,' said the driver.

The driver was going very fast, as there were very few cars

on the road. In two hours, we were in Ngundu. When I looked in the back of the lorry, I could see my friends piled up together with their heads lowered as they tried to avoid the strong cold winds. I felt sorry for them, but being in the back of a lorry was far better than walking.

'So why are you on the run?' asked the driver.

'Politics,' I replied.

'So you must be the unlucky Chematama supporters,' said the driver, laughing.

I didn't like the nickname they gave to our leader, Morgan Tsvangirai. But they were right; he really did have big cheeks.

'Don't say that about the future president of this country,' said Happiness.

'How can that happen when you, his supporters who are supposed to vote for him, are fleeing the country?' said the driver.

'What makes you think we are MDC supporters?' I asked.

'It's happening everywhere. In Lutumba, most MDC supporters have fled to South Africa. I've lived here a long time. I have witnessed things I never imagined would happen in Zimbabwe, especially in this day and age,' said the driver.

'That's why they say that politics is a dirty game,' said Happiness as she turned around to look at the back of the lorry.

Ever since we had got into the lorry, she had kept glancing in the back, obviously worried about her husband. Titus and Happiness made me laugh. I wondered if they had ever lived far from each other. I don't know what she would have done if it had been Titus who had been left behind instead of Peter. I think she would have killed herself.

'You are already missing him' I teased her.

'What are you talking about?' asked Happiness, smiling.

'You are worried that your husband might fall off, aren't you?' I laughed.

'I don't know what that man has done to me. Whatever it is, it must be very strong. I can't imagine my life without him. He means everything to me,' Happiness replied, still looking back.

'I like it, you guys seem to be deeply in love with each other.'

'You're right. We have been for twenty-nine years. We met in 1979, when Titus came to Mozambique to train for the liberation struggle. Ever since then, we have been like trousers and a belt, inseparable.'

'I didn't know you'd been to Mozambique as well,' I said, surprised.

'I grew up in Mutare and my father's job was to help the youth cross into Mozambique for military training. A sell-out reported him to Ian Smith's soldiers, actually. Luckily, the news got to my father in time and we escaped the night the soldiers had planned to come for our family. I was twenty-two years old at the time and, on getting to Mozambique, I was recruited and trained as a cook and entertainer for the soldiers who were based there. Many soldiers came, leaving after their training, but I stayed.

'My parents also left for the battleground. Five years later, I met a handsome boy who introduced himself as Tito, a nickname for Titus. It was love at first sight. I knew straight away he was the man I wanted to spend the rest of my life with.

We started going out and our love grew stronger each day.

'A few months later, I received the sad news that the two groups which my father and mother had gone with had perished. It was one of the most painful and difficult times for me. I didn't want to believe it was true, but Titus was there for me. He helped me get through the ordeal. I was glad that he never got the chance to go and fight, because I didn't want to lose another person who was so dear to me.

'After the war, I was optimistic that maybe I was going to see my parents alive - maybe the news I received was false - but they never showed up. Titus helped me search for them but we never found them. I finally accepted that they had very likely died in the war.

'So you see, that man back there is all I have. We have never been able to have any kids, so he is my mother, my father, my husband and my child.'

'I didn't know you didn't have any children. I'm sorry. I always thought your children were probably in Harare or working somewhere far away,' I said.

'It's OK, I accepted a long time ago that I would never have any children,' she said.

I could see that her eyes had welled up with tears. There is nothing so heartbreaking for a woman as to not be able to hold your own child in your arms. Losing her parents in such a horrible way must have been very traumatic for her. Titus was truly all she had and it was clear that she was glad he had stuck by her through it all.

I noticed the driver wiping his eyes. I looked at him and saw that he had been touched by her story as well. He didn't say anything, however. He kept his eyes glued on the road.

After driving for more than two hours, we passed through Mwenezi, where I dozed off.

'Nyasha! Nyasha! Nyasha!' I heard Happiness shouting my name as she shook me.

'What?' I replied, trying to focus my eyes as I woke up. Happiness had just awoken me from a terrible dream. The rape by those barbarians was continuously haunting me. It seemed every time I fell asleep, I relived the rape in my dreams. *Will this ever stop?*

'You freaked us out,' said the driver, a shocked look on his face.

'You were screaming. I was afraid you might try to jump out of the car,' said Happiness.

'I had a terrible dream' I replied, wiping sweat off my forehead.

'What did you dream about? Was it scary, Mum?' asked my daughter.

I didn't know how to answer my little girl's question. It was a dream I would never tell anyone about, especially not her. I could see by Happiness's expression that she had worked out what the dream was about.

'We will be in Lutumbe in ten minutes' time,' said the driver.

'I thought you were taking us to Beitbridge?'

'There were some complications in taking you all the way there. I'm sorry.'

I sighed, somewhat saddened. 'Well, that was still quick,' I said trying to steer away from Sheila's question.

'You were asleep. If you had been awake, you would have seen how long it was,' said Happiness.

I wished he could have taken us all the way to Beitbridge. But still, I was very grateful for the help he had given us. Our legs had at least rested. He had fed us and had brought us closer to our destination. For that we were very grateful; there weren't many people who would do that for a group of strangers.

After about fifteen more minutes, the driver pulled off, passing some shops, and stopped.

'This is my home town. I will be turning left up there. It is the furthest I can get you. You'll have to continue with your journey on foot,' said the driver.

'Come on girls,' I said as I looked at Happiness, who was knocking on the back window, getting her husband's attention.

'Sir, I don't know how to thank you for what you have done for us. We are very grateful to you,' I said.

'It's OK. I wish you all the best in South Africa.'

'Thank you,' replied Happiness. We all jumped out, including those in the back of the lorry, and everyone came to thank him.

'We don't have anything to offer you. But we promise that we will never forget you and we will always ask God to remember you. We forgot to ask you your name,' said Titus.

'Chenjerai Mombeshora,' replied the driver.

'I'm Titus and this is my lovely wife Happiness,' said Titus, gesturing towards her.

'Nice to meet you all and I wish you a safe journey,' said the driver.

'Same to you and again, thank you,' said Titus.

'Now that we know you and we know where to find you, we will come to thank you properly in the future,' said Edwin.

'It is my pleasure. If it were my car, I would have taken you all the way to Beitbridge, but my boss always checks the mileage. I'm sorry I didn't mention it sooner.'

'It is OK man, this is great. You have given us a lot of help. Thank you again,' said Wellington.

'All the best to you all. God be with you, I have to go now,' said the driver.

'Thank you,' we said in unison, sounding like a choir.

We all watched and waved goodbye as he drove off.

CHAPTER 10

We looked for a nice place to rest, knowing that Beitbridge was now just a day or two away. Everyone was now very eager to get to the border. We didn't wait for it to get dark as we had before. In the afternoon, we began walking again. This time, we had energy in our step, as we knew we were now very close to the Zimbabwean border with South Africa. We had walked 250 kilometres in less than two weeks, addition to the distance we were carried in the truck.

The next day, May 3, we arrived in Beitbridge. It was exactly as we had expected it to be. It was crowded and busy, which was always how people who had been there described it. I was surprised by how many people appeared to live on the streets. I saw some in the street corners and in other random locations, apparently going where they felt it was safe.

Prostitutes and thieves were abundant. It was difficult to trust anyone in such a place, especially with what we had gone through in Nyamutumbu. I feared for my little girls. People here were smart, and they could tell just by looking at you if you were from the area or not. We were dirty, our clothes had been torn in the bushes, and we did not smell nice at all. I began to wonder if this helped, as it appeared to turn thieves away from us. We had no problems from them, most likely because they figured out we wouldn't have the valuables or money they were looking for.

People in Beitbridge would do anything to survive. I wondered why they didn't all try to cross over the border, as people said it was easy to make money in South Africa.

'Let's find somewhere to rest, and then tomorrow we'll see how we can cross the border,' said Titus.

'Can't we go today?' asked Wellington.

Titus sighed. 'I know you all can't wait to cross over but it's best we rest today. We'll have energy and clear minds to figure out how to cross tomorrow.'

We managed to find a very nice, quiet place to rest our tired legs. At night, the men went and looked for their own place to sleep. I couldn't wait for the next day to arrive, as I was very eager to get to South Africa. I didn't really feel safe in Beitbridge. Once in South Africa, we would be far away from people who knew we were MDC supporters. Peter would then be my next priority. *It's been many days now since I last saw him. I miss him so much. I must find a way to get him here, to rejoin our family. If he's alive.*

In the morning, we were woken up by the screams of Zvanyadza, who had had the same nightmare we all shared. Her voice rang in the soprano range as she screamed. Zvanyadza and Tafara had been our village entertainers. Tafara played *mbira* (thump piano) and Zvanyadza sang. She was blessed with a very beautiful voice, which clearly stood out in everything she did, whether she was singing or shouting. As a couple, they provided entertainment at all village gatherings, be they political or social. They had one son who had followed in their footsteps and was always on the road travelling with a band as the *mbira* player.

Zvanyadza looked scared and upset. I watched as she ran her fingers through her long brown braids, which matched her baby-soft brown skin. Our past was now haunting us more and more. No matter where we went, the events of that sad night were always with us. No one was comfortable talking about their nightmares, but we knew they were all about the rape ordeal. We didn't talk about it, but we knew. Every time I slept, I could see the faces of the militia members cheering each other on as they took turns forcing themselves on me. Would these memories always be a burden I would have to bear?

Two hours later, the men joined us and we started planning how to cross the border. They had done some research before they came to us, as they were already acquainted with the various ways of crossing over.

'400 rands? That's too much!' I said, surprised by what I had heard the bus drivers were demanding to help us enter South Africa.

'Is that for all of us?' asked Zvanyadza.

'That's for one,' replied Wellington.

'That's too much!' said Zvanyadza.

'I agree with you, it is ridiculous, but that's what they want,' said Titus.

I couldn't believe what I was hearing. I wished we could find another generous man like Chenjerai Mombeshora to help us cross the border. People like that were not easy to come by. We knew we couldn't go back, so we had to try everything within our power to get to the other side.

'If it were for all of us, that price would have been reasonable,' said Ruramai.

'Still, we couldn't have afforded it. If we change the few Zimbabwean dollars we have, they wouldn't amount to 200 rands,' Titus said, looking frustrated.

'How about the plan the other man mentioned?' asked Tafara.

'I'm not up for that one, it's too dangerous,' replied Wellington.

'What is this other plan you are talking about?' asked Gertrude.

'We talked to this other fat man on our way here who said many people swim across the Limpopo river to get into South Africa,' Wellington replied.

'Isn't the river too wide?' I asked, trying to get a better picture of the situation.

'There are a lot of people who have crossed the border that way, but yes, the river is wide,' said Edwin.

'Are you sure about that?' asked Wellington.

'That is what the fat man said' replied Brighton.

'What if he was lying to us? I'm not going anywhere near that river,' said Wellington. 'There are crocodiles. It's too dangerous.'

'Where are you going to get the 400 rands from, then?' I asked.

'I am a man. I will see what I can do. I'm sure I can find work somewhere,' replied Wellington.

'We have all worked together as a team up to this point. It's important we stick together for the rest of the journey,' said Titus.

'If we all stick together, it will be more difficult to raise the money we require. I think we've hit the point where we all have to be on our own. Every man for himself' said Wellington.

'We all said that we are going to South Africa together when we started this journey. As long as we haven't reached our destination, we should all stick together,' said Titus.

We all sat there in silence, wondering if there was something else we could do to raise the required money. All in all, we needed 4,800 rands. That was a lot of money. We didn't know how long it would take us to get that kind of money if we stayed in Beitbridge. I then understood why there were so many prostitutes and thieves around. They were all probably trying to raise the money to cross over to South Africa.

'I think the only option on the table for us is to swim,' said Titus.

'I say it would be better if we wait and try to raise the money,' said Wellington.

'I think it is best that we all stick together, but I can't force anyone to stay if they don't want to. I am going to swim and anyone up for it can join me,' said Titus.

We all looked at him in shock by what he had just said. I could see that he was determined. I had never seen such a brave man in my life. He was not scared of anything. His military training showed through more and more. I was glad that we had someone of his calibre in our midst. He was indeed a risk taker, but I wondered if he could see the dangers of what he was embarking on.

'You can count me out of this, there's no way I'm swimming across a crocodile-infested river,' said Wellington.

I knew I only had one choice. There was no way I was going

to raise that kind of money. All in all, I would need to raise 800 rands if I followed Wellington's plan. I made up my mind to take a risk and go with Titus' plan.

I was especially worried about Sheila. She could swim, but I wasn't sure if she could make it to the other side of that big river.

One of the good things about growing up in the rural area of Zimbabwe was the training you would get at a tender age. At five, there were so many things that my daughter could do that other kids of the same age who had grown up in the urban areas could not. She could sweep the house, wash the dishes and cook, which I had begun teaching her to do.

I looked at the undecided faces of our group. I wished there had been another option for us, but there was none. Even Happiness wasn't sure if her husband had made the right decision. But, after all the things I had gone through over the past few days, could I not conquer anything? As I thought about what kind of strength I had, I felt I could do it. I could cross the river. I was up for the challenge. If I were to die, it simply meant my time had come. Chiwoniso's death had given me a new perceptive. My best friend thought she was running away from death, not knowing she was actually walking towards it. I knew I could be doing either with such a decision.

'I'm coming with you,' I said, standing up.

'Me too,' said Edwin.

'Me too,' echoed Brighton.

It was as if my boldness had suddenly inspired everyone as they all stood up in support of Titus.

'Do you think these little girls will be able to swim across that wide river?' asked Wellington, looking concerned.

'We'll help them when they get tired,' replied Titus.

Everyone except Wellington voted for the swimming option. There was no need for us to waste much time. It was best we went to inspect the river ourselves.

We took our belongings and began heading towards the river. It was sad that Wellington had decided to leave on his own. He looked at us sadly and walked away.

'All the best, guys!' he shouted as he waved goodbye.

'Same to you!' replied Titus. 'See you on the other side.'

After walking a short distance, we arrived at the river. I panicked when I saw how wide it was, seeing the large distance we had to cross – it must have been 150 metres across. The fear of crocodiles gripped me.

We walked down the river, looking for the ideal place to cross, which we hoped was the same spot many others used to cross the river. After wandering around, anxiously trying to locate the crossing, we found it. The shoreline jutted out at two points, creating a fairly hidden cove where we could get into the water without anyone on other parts of the shore noticing. Our hearts fell when we saw that crocodiles were not very far from it. We stood there wondering what to do. We knew any sort of noise in the water would alert the crocodiles to our presence. Once they knew we were in the water, we would be done for.

'I'll go and distract the crocodiles with the dogs' said Titus. 'As I get the dogs barking, all of you cross the river. You have to be gentle when you get into the water to avoid splashing.'

'What about you?' asked a worried-looking Happiness.

'Don't worry about me, I'll make it. I will meet you on the other side,' replied Titus.

We all looked away as the couple hugged and kissed. The shy little girls covered their faces. I realised the gravity of what we were planning to do. What if one of the girls was attacked? Could we live with our decision? What if something happened to a couple who lived and died for each other? This was all happening so rapidly. Perhaps we weren't thinking clearly, or were attempting to cross the river too close to the crocodiles. I was hoping we could perhaps postpone the crossing until the next day, or wait for the crocodiles to move a bit further down the river. Titus didn't agree. He didn't want us to wait. All he wanted was to get to South Africa as quickly as possible. Here, we were in danger. There, we'd be safe. At least, that was our hope.

'I love you,' said Happiness.

'I love you too,' replied Titus.

'Please be careful.' They embraced for some time, not willing to let go.

'I have to go now,' said Titus. Happiness looked worried.

'I will be fine, don't worry.'

He pulled away from Happiness, gave her hand a quick squeeze and turned away from us. He took the dogs and walked in the direction in which we had seen the crocodiles. I could see Happiness shaking. After what she had explained to me in the lorry, I understood why. They were very much in love. If it were Sheila or Peter taking that kind of a risk, I would have behaved the same way.

We waited for Titus' signal. After what felt like hours, we heard him drop something into the water, causing the dogs to bark. We knew that the dogs had spotted the crocodiles and we made our move. This was the signal we were waiting for.

Gently we got into the river, walking where it wasn't too deep and swimming once we could no longer stand. We kept as quiet as possible as we moved deeper and deeper into the river. We didn't care whether our handbags or other belongings got wet. Getting to the other side was the only thing that mattered.

Esther and Sheila were struggling to keep up as we began to swim. Edwin and Tafara assisted them throughout the journey. When we saw the shore finally appear, we realised we had made it safely to the other side. The sense of relief was overwhelming. We had made it to South Africa, free and far away from Mugabe's cruel militia.

We cried and hugged each other, amazed that we made it across safely after such a dangerous crossing. One of us, however, was not smiling. It took us a moment to realise that Happiness was not celebrating. She was still worried about her husband. The danger Titus was about to put himself in, all to allow us a safe crossing, became a reality.

I followed Happiness's gaze, searching for Titus across the river. As we were all focused on crossing the river, we weren't sure whether Titus was able to keep himself away from the crocodiles. But after a few moments I was relieved to see Titus and the dogs walking towards the place from where we had crossed.

Titus took the four dogs and, with some rope he must have found on the shoreline, tied them to a nearby tree. I was sure the thought of parting with the dogs was difficult. They had been a great help to us in finding food. More than that, the men had spent years training the dogs to be both companions and assistants in their everyday life. But I knew, as I'm sure the men did, that Titus had no choice - crossing the river with dogs would attract too much attention. The crocodiles would have them in minutes.

Titus returned to the edge of the river, seemingly deliberating on the best time to cross. Eventually, we saw him gently descend into the river. Happiness let out a small moan and grabbed my hand, grasping it tightly. We all watched anxiously as he slowly swam towards us. There was no splashing or any noise at all. No one passing by would have known that there was someone in the river.

My grip on Happiness's hand loosened as I felt a sense of relief. Titus knew what he was doing. He was our guide, our counsellor, our leader. He had the knowledge and skill to get us here after such life-changing events. He would be able to cross the river. He would return safely to us and guide us to a happy life in South Africa.

My gaze wandered as I allowed relief to wash over me, but it was short-lived. Happiness squeezed my hand harder and gasped. I focused my attention on Titus and saw that he was attempting to swim faster without making any noise. Confusion set in until I looked to the opposite shoreline and saw the dogs. Three of the dogs were still tied to the tree. The fourth dog had wiggled its way through the rope and was at the water's edge, whimpering for Titus. If the dog got in the water, the noise would alert the crocodiles to Titus' presence.

Titus was almost at the shoreline. Some of the men quietly made their way to the edge of the shore to help him stand up if needed. Edwin noiselessly picked up a large branch nearby, clearly preparing for what we all knew could happen. We all eyed the dog anxiously, praying it wouldn't follow Titus into the river. But it was not enough. I closed my eyes as the dog jumped into the water. The noise wasn't horribly loud, but we all knew it was loud enough to catch the crocodiles' attention. I opened my eyes to see the crocodiles rapidly closing the space between them and the dog.

The relief I felt that the crocodiles would not head for Titus was brief.

'No! Oh, God, no!' I heard Happiness groan.

One crocodile had broken away from the others. It was heading full speed towards Titus, who was only a few feet away from the shoreline, swimming as quickly as he could. But the crocodile was faster. His hands hit the shoreline and, as he lifted one leg out of the water, the men grabbing his arms to pull him up, he was quickly jerked back, screaming in agony as he sank back into the water.

The men ran forward. I tried to see what was happening. I moaned in despair. The crocodile had clamped onto Titus' other leg, pulling him into the water. I knew, as did everyone, that a crocodile's bite was nearly impossible to break. Edwin had already jumped into the water with the branch he had found and was hitting the crocodile repeatedly as both the crocodile and Titus thrashed in the water. Some of the other men found branches and ran in as well, joining Edwin in a desperate attempt to distract the crocodile enough to save Titus.

Happiness was sobbing. She turned into my shoulder and buried her head in my neck, wailing out,

'Titus! Titus! Titus! Oh my Titus! Oh my God, tell me this is not happening to me!'

I wrapped my arms around her, watching in horror the scene in front of me. The struggle continued. I could see the blood running through the water. As the men continued battling the crocodile, Edwin swung a final time and made contact with one of the crocodile's eyes. That was enough. As though in shock, the crocodile released Titus and jerked its head back. The others quickly grabbed Titus and dragged him out of the river with Edwin walking behind them, facing the crocodile and holding the branch up, ready to strike back if the crocodile attacked again.

The crocodile watched for a moment and then swam away. I thanked God in a silent prayer for such a miraculous blessing.

Happiness broke away from me as the men dragged Titus further inland. We all followed, with both Brighton and I swooping up Esther and Sheila. We all wanted to get away from the river as quickly as possible.

'How bad is it?' I inquired as we got closer.

Gertrude was the only one who answered. 'It's hard to tell. There is so much blood.'

Happiness was at Titus' side, attempting to clean the wounds with her hands. The bites were deep; there was no question.

The men were debating over what to do and how best to treat him. We had no idea if we were near a hospital and, even if we were, we had no idea how far we needed to walk. Tafara raised his voice and said, 'We need to make a tourniquet.'

This silenced everyone. They stared at him, unsure of what he was trying, or meant, to say.

Tafara repeated, 'We need to make a tourniquet. I saw my

father do it once on one of the men in our village. He had accidentally cut himself on his leg. The blood wouldn't stop. A tourniquet will help stop the bleeding.'

There was a very brief moment of silence when Happiness spoke up, a tone of determination in her voice. 'Do it.'

Tafara nodded his head once, bent down to pick up a small stick, and walked over to Titus.

He looked down at Titus, who was shaking with pain and shock.

'I need a thick piece of cloth. Quickly.'

Gertrude stepped forward. One of the long sleeves on her shirt had a large tear in it near the bicep. She pulled hard at the sleeve and handed the lower portion to Tafara.

Tafara took the cloth and very gently raised Titus' injured leg. He took the cloth and wrapped it around the back of his leg, softly setting the leg back down as he brought the two sides of the cloth together. He then picked up the stick, tying it to the cloth ends, and began twisting. Titus yelled in pain as Tafara continued twisting the stick. Happiness looked at him with a harsh glare.

'Tafara Kaseke, you are hurting him!'

'I am sorry, Happiness, but it is the only way to stop the bleeding. The only way he will live is if we stop the bleeding.'

Gertrude stepped forward. 'We need to cover his wounds. Quickly, gather some of the bigger leaves you can find.'

The men dispersed through the jungle and came back shortly with various leaves. Gertrude tenderly wrapped Titus' leg with the leaves, tying them off with some of the longer grass close by.

CHAPTER TEN

I couldn't even express the gratitude I felt that Titus was alive. Without his bravery, without his skills, without his knowledge, I knew it would have been very hard for us to get where we were. I just prayed he would survive.

CHAPTER 11

We began our journey again, with a man on each side of Titus, helping to carry him as he attempted to walk on one leg. *If you had done the same for Peter, he would have made it. If you had helped him walk, he would have been right here next to me.* I was shocked at the animosity I began to feel towards the men as I watched them take care of Titus. But I reminded myself of what they had done in taking care of Sheila and me. Could I blame them for escaping that school without looking back, when they were trying to save the lives of their families?

We walked for hours, but it was clear that Titus was struggling. Happiness kept her hand on his back, keeping in contact with him the entire time. We walked further, but one of the men decided we needed to rest. Both of Titus' feet were dragging and he appeared to be on the verge of passing out from the pain.

We all sat on the ground, grateful for a rest.

'You ladies stay here,' said Tafara as he stood up. 'We are going to see if we can get fruits or anything we can eat.'

We looked on as the men marched away. I prayed and hoped that they would get something to give us a bit of energy and something to give Titus what he needed to heal. Happiness was right at her husband's side as she and some of the other ladies helped redress the wounds.

I glanced back to Sheila and Esther, who were holding hands as they played with some rocks they had found. They had been fairly silent through our journey. They were frightened by what they had seen and clung closely to Brighton and I as we had walked.

'Mum, I need to go to the bathroom,' said Sheila as she stood up and walked towards me.

I looked around to see if there was anywhere suitable to take her.

'Come on then, follow me,' I said as I led her away from the ladies.

I decided to take her further away because I didn't want the smell to irritate the others. Esther followed. The little girls were inseparable. As we walked, I looked for a suitable place far enough away from the group. Once we were far enough away, I pointed to a small tree and told Sheila to go behind the tree. I looked on as Esther, who stood next to me, waited for Sheila to finish. I noticed an odd smell in the air. I sniffed the air once more, noticing the potato-like smell, and felt a flood of memories rush back to me. My feet became weak and I started shaking. I felt I was about to faint.

Sheila was kneeling behind a *Phyllanthus reticulatus* tree, the same tree I hid behind when Fadzi and Adamson came after Peter. I looked at the tree, with its thinly textured leaves, brown berry-like fruits and green-yellow flowers. It brought all the events of that sad night back. I could see them kicking my unconscious husband. As I looked through the branches and leaves, I could see the faces of Adamson and Fadzi as they looked at the motionless body of Peter. 'Is he dead? Is he dead?

98

Is he dead? Is he dead?' Adamson's question played in my head again and again. *Is he dead? He can't be. Peter is a fighter, he must be alive.*

'Put your hands up now! Now!' I heard a male voice shouting, making me jump.

The voice was unfamiliar. The first thought that came to my mind, the nightmare that reappeared, was the memory of the rape. That was the last time I had heard a male voice I didn't recognise address us.

Sheila had finished and both the girls had run over to me, clinging to my legs. I pulled them back and squatted down, getting eye level to them.

'Stay here, girls. Hide behind this tree and whatever you do, don't come out unless someone from our group comes to get you.'

'No! Don't leave me again!' Sheila whimpered, clutching my shirt in her hand.

'You have to be brave, Sheila. You and Esther both have to be brave. I promise you, I will be back. Promise me you'll stay hidden.'

Sheila looked at me with tears in her big brown eyes. 'I promise,' Esther nodded in agreement, taking Sheila's hand.

I stood up slowly and began walking, stepping softly through the foliage of the jungle. I followed the direction the voice had come from and quickly squatted down behind some bushes and, looking through the bushes, saw three men holding machetes and knives. I could see the shaking bodies of Ruramai, Happiness, Zvanyadza, and Gertrude, obviously confused by what was happening.

'Are you deaf? Put your hands where we can see them!' one of the men shouted.

I couldn't believe what was happening. This was our promised land, a land of peace, milk and honey. A place we thought we would be safe. I didn't expect any attacks now that we were in South Africa. *Maybe Mugabe's militias followed us all the way here*, I thought.

'Empty your handbags and pockets now,' shouted one of the men. The ladies slowly emptied all of their pockets. One of the men glanced over, seeing that Happiness was standing over something. He walked over, swinging his machete. I heard Titus, in a weakened voice, attempt to yell, saying, 'Get away from us. We've done nothing to you.'

The man began laughing. 'That is where you're wrong. You have what we need.' He bent down and, swinging his hand back, hit Titus' head with the handle of the machete. I heard a loud crack and a shriek from Happiness.

One of the other men continued. 'Anyone wearing a necklace or a watch remove it and put it down now!'

Happiness was sobbing as she began removing some of her jewellery. The other women did the same.

'Hurry up, we don't have all day!' screamed one of them.

I looked around carefully, trying to see everything I could without revealing myself. The men were going through the contents of the handbags, obviously selecting what they thought would get them quick cash. They were whispering amongst themselves, clearly planning something.

They stood up. The man who hit Titus began yelling,

'Take off your clothes, now!'

I froze. My worst fears were coming true. I was sure all of the women's worst fears were coming true at that moment as well. I didn't know what to do. The fear of being raped again kept me frozen in place. But the thought of allowing these women, who had become like family, to be raped again sickened me as well. I could see some of the ladies slowly undressing.

'This is taking too long,' yelled the man with the machete. He walked up to Happiness and put the machete to her neck. 'Hurry up, or else she dies.'

'Take off everything!' screamed one of them. Their patience was running thin.

I heard a loud slap and saw Ruramai holding her face, screaming.

'Hurry up! We don't have the whole day!' shouted one of the men.

The women still weren't fully undressed, the fear vividly apparent in their eyes. I couldn't stand it. I grabbed a branch I thought I could swing, preparing to try and save my sisters.

'Lie down! Quickly!' the thugs shouted.

They must have decided to undress the women themselves. Just then, I heard a rustling in the bushes. Ruramai's scream had alerted the men and I saw Edwin, Brighton, and Tafara running towards the ladies.

'Hey! What's going on?' Edwin shouted as the men ran towards the commotion.

The thugs, on hearing and seeing Edwin, Brighton and Tafara, ran away. I thanked God that the men made it in time. They had approached the women, helping them get their clothing and belongings. They were badly shaken up, and rightly so. Brighton saw me stand up and ran over.

'Are you OK?' inquired Brighton.

'Yes. I took the girls to the bathroom and heard the men come. I'm so glad you came in time. Let's go get the girls.'

We walked over to the tree where I had left Esther and Sheila. I saw Sheila's face glance around the trunk. When she saw it was Brighton and I, she ran straight into my arms. Esther did the same with Brighton.

We walked back to the rest of the group. Titus had woken up and, luckily, appeared to be all right. Happiness was feeding him some of the food the men had brought back.

'Please, let's get out of this place before something worse happens,' I said as soon as I got to everyone.

Brighton, with sympathy in his eyes, responded, 'We will. But we need to eat first. Everyone is weak from our journey. Do not worry, we will protect you.'

We ate quickly and left as soon as Titus felt well enough to stand.

As we were walking, I began thinking about what had just happened. We were not as safe as we thought we would be after arriving in South Africa. The area we were in had proved to be dangerous. I wanted us to get away as quickly as possible. We clearly did not know the area or the type of people that patrolled here. No one seemed to know the way we were supposed to go. Titus was exhausted and weak but would try to guide us when he could.

Titus was good at making quick and sound decisions. He had also been very instrumental in our welfare, making sure we were always cheerful and that there was plenty of food at all times. Just a few hours after his injury, we were already greatly missing his constant guidance. We all looked at each other constantly, not knowing the direction to take.

After we had stopped, Happiness moved in front of Titus, trying to get him to focus on her. We were in unfamiliar territory, not knowing the area or what the next best step would be. We needed his leadership now more than ever.

'Which direction should we take my husband?' asked Happiness in a gentle voice.

Titus moaned, but could do no more.

We all looked around, checking for roads, footsteps or anything that could lead us to a place where we could ask for help. We saw nothing.

Brighton stood up, catching all of our attention. 'Follow me,' he said. I was relieved, knowing there was someone who was appeared to be willing to fill Titus' shoes.

'Are you sure you know where you are taking us?' asked Edwin, a look of apprehension on his face.

'No. But it is better than just standing here, waiting for the lions to come and eat us,' replied Brighton.

'This is a blind man leading the blind,' teased Tafara.

'Shut up, Tafara. If you are blind, don't assume everyone here is blind. Regardless, we need to get help for Titus, who is the only other person willing and able to lead us,' said Brighton.

We stood up, following our new self-appointed leader. He was trying to do all he could to cheer us up so that we would forget our current situation, forget we were stuck in a country we didn't know and not knowing where we were heading. Brighton had obviously learned a few things from Titus.

Our walk on the South African side was the most difficult and painful for us. Because of the fear we felt after what had just happened to us, we never rested. We had eaten only a few fruits and had no water. The man and the dogs, which had played a vital role in hunting for us, were no longer able to help. The little girls were tired, hungry and crying.

The men helped by carrying the girls at times, but they could only carry them for so long before they became tired. Slowly we kept pushing, forcing our tired legs to continue. No one was talking. I was exhausted. I felt I would faint if we had to continue any further.

I was relieved when we came to some fields. It was obvious people lived nearby. The sizes of the fields proved that these were farms. Our spirits rose and we felt energy bubbling up slowly inside of us again.

We started the hunt for the houses of the farm owners. After walking for a time in now near darkness, we heard the barking of dogs and knew that houses were nearby. We kept walking in the direction of the dogs until we started seeing some lights – a house.

We were surprised by how beautiful the house was. It was a two-storey building surrounded by green lawns and beautiful flowers. As we moved closer, the dogs started barking more and more, making us nervous. I wondered how many dogs the farmer had – he was clearly rich.

One of the windows on the second floor was open, and someone was pointing a torch at us through it. He spoke in a language which none of us understood.

'What the hell is he saying?' asked Zvanyadza, exhausted from the journey.

'I have absolutely no idea' replied Brighton.

'What language is that?' I asked.

'It sounds like Afrikaans' replied Tafara.

The man disappeared from the window and a few minutes later he appeared out of the front door. He walked right in front of us and pointed a huge gun in our faces.

We were all shocked, not expecting this type of greeting.

'Who are you and what is it that you want?' asked the man, now in English.

'We are from Zimbabwe! We are running away from the cruel Mugabe militia! Please, we beg you to help us!' shouted Brighton, raising his hands in the air.

'How many are you?' asked the man.

Brighton looked around as he counted.

'We are nine adults and two children,' replied Brighton.

He paused for a moment. '*Mira* [Wait]!' he said in our mother tongue as he hurried back to the house.

We all hesitated, cautiously optimistic as we heard him trying to say more Shona words.

'Who the hell is this guy?' asked Edwin to the rest of the group.

'I wonder who has taught him our language,' I said.

'He must have some Zimbabwean workers here,' said Gertrude.

The man came back with two dogs and the gun still in his hands. He was a white man with a red beard and looked like he was in his sixties.

'Hello everyone,' said the white man.

'Hi,' we all muttered quietly, still nervous.

'My name is Tom Volek and I am the owner of this farm. I can see you are all tired so let's find you some place to rest. We will then talk in the morning. Come with me. *Shamwari* [friends], follow me.'

A laugh slipped from Happiness at the mention of the word *shamwari*, whether from exhaustion or relief I couldn't tell. We followed our new friend as he took us to some rundown huts a distance from his house. As we got closer, I could see they were in bad shape; the huts in our village looked far more beautiful than these. They didn't look like they were suitable for any human beings to live in. There were holes in the roof and the walls were falling apart. But none of it mattered. All we wanted was a place to sleep; somewhere we knew we would be safe. This was far better than sleeping under trees and rocks. Mr. Volek went and knocked on the door of one of the huts.

'Zivai! Zivai! Zivai! It's me, Tom. Open up!' he shouted as he banged on the door.

'OK boss, I'm coming!' a gruff male voice shouted from inside the ugly hut.

The old door squeaked open. We saw a man poke his head out. He was old, tall and slim and had a white goatee beard.

'I have got your brothers and sisters here, Zivai,' said Mr. Volek.

'Oh I see, another lot,' replied the man, yawning.

'All you men, I will leave you in this man's hands. He will answer everything you would like to know about this place,' said Mr. Volek. 'And Miss,' he said, turning to Happiness, 'He tends to those on the farm who become injured. He will tend to your husband while you rest.' He turned back around, waving his hand in the air briefly. 'See you in the morning, men.'

'Thank you sir; see you in the morning,' replied Brighton as the other men helped Titus into the hut.

'All you ladies come with me,' said Mr. Volek.

We followed him to the next squalid hut. We waited and watched as he banged on a door, which looked like it was about to fall in.

'Mazvita! Mazvita! Mazvita! Open up, it's me, Mr. Volek,' he shouted.

'Uuumh!' we heard a female voice yawning inside the hut.

The door made a screeching sound as it opened to reveal a short, slim, ugly woman with a shaven head. I wondered if there were any healthy-looking people on this farm. *They must work extra hard and get little food*, I thought.

'Sorry to disturb you, Mazvita. I have brought you some friends,' said Mr. Volek.

'OK,' said the sleepy Mazvita.

'Ladies, make yourselves at home. Mazvita here will take good care of you' said Mr. Volek. 'We will talk in the morning.'

'Thank you sir' we all muttered.

'I will see you in the morning,' said Mr. Volek and he went back to his beautiful house.

'Come in,' said Mazvita as she waved us in. She was light in complexion and looked as if she was in her late forties. The room was very clean and tidy but had no bed, which meant she must sleep on the floor. Her clothes were nicely folded and placed in a corner. On the other corner lay another lady whose snoring sounded like a frog croaking. I wondered how Mr. Volek's banging on the door had not awakened her. She must have been very tired.

'You must have walked from the river,' said Mazvita. 'Have you had anything to eat recently?'

'We are starving and thirsty too,' replied Ruramai.

'Let me go and quickly prepare something for you, then,' said Mazvita.

'You don't have to, my sister; we can wait till morning. If you can please just get us some water,' said Zvanyadza.

'I know what it is like to walk from that river. If not for you, I will at least make something for these little girls. I can't let them go to sleep on an empty stomach,' replied Mazvita as she stood up to go to the kitchen.

'I would like to come and give you a hand, if it's OK with you,' I said.

'As would I,' echoed Gertrude.

I wanted to take advantage of time alone with Mazvita and ask her a little about the farm. The farm owner had seemed very nice, and if the pay was good, then I thought I could stay for a while.

'It's OK, let's go,' said Mazvita.

'You girls stay here with Auntie Zvanyadza. I will be back soon with lots of food,' I said as I stroked Sheila's hair.

She and Esther had already snuggled next to each other, lying down, looking exhausted. The girls didn't reply. I could see they didn't have the strength to talk.

CHAPTER 12

Gertrude and I followed Mazvita to the kitchen. There was electricity, so we were able to cook with electric stoves rather than firewood as we were used to in the rural areas. There was also a big fridge, which kept all the food fresh. She took meat, vegetables and tomatoes out of it.

'Won't the meat take too long to cook?' I asked. 'We don't want to take much of your time. We know you must want to rest as well.'

'We don't mind having just the vegetables,' said Gertrude.

'These are chicken livers, they will be very quick to cook,' said Mazvita.

'OK, that's fine then,' I said.

'Where is the maize flour?' asked Gertrude.

She took out everything we wanted to use to cook. Gertrude started preparing the *sadza* while I cut the vegetables and Mazvita fried the chicken livers.

'So, you guys must be MDC supporters,' said Mazvita.

'How did you know that?' I asked.

'This seems to be the first stop for everyone running away from Mugabe's militia,' replied Mazvita.

'Really? There must be a lot of Zimbabweans here then,' I said

'You must have been here for a long time to be trusted this much by that white farmer' said Gertrude.

'I would say so. Many people come and go. I'm one of the few who has stuck around.'

'Did you run away from Mugabe as well?' I asked, looking towards her as she worked on the livers.

'No. I have been here for three years now. I came here before all the political violence started.'

'They must be taking good care of you to stay for that long,' said Gertrude.

Mazvita scoffed loudly. 'Not really. There are many obstacles to overcome in trying to leave this place. Now that you are here, you will see it for yourself. I don't have anywhere else to go, otherwise I would have gone a long time ago.'

Gertrude and I looked at each other, confusion clearly written on our faces. After a moment of silence, Gertrude spoke up,

'We are just passing by. We don't intend to stay here for long.'

'Do you honestly think it's going to be easy for you to just walk away from this farm?' said Mazvita.

'What do you mean?' I asked.

'Did you not find it odd that a white man is the owner of this farm, that he was the one to greet you and take you in? There is a lot of work here and that white guy you saw will not be happy to see you leave. You're cheap labour for him. He's trying to make as much money with as little expense as possible,' said Mazvita.

I felt my spirits drop considerably. After everything I'd been through, after everything the group had been through, we had ended up at a farm with a tyrant controlling it, holding us captive. I had left our home, my husband, everything behind for freedom. And now I was a captive.

'I don't care whether he is happy or not. I can't stay here,' said Gertrude. 'I have a brother in Mpumalanga Province and he can get me something better to do. Why should I suffer at this farm when I have somewhere else to go? Why should anyone feel like they need to stay?'

'So many people who have said the same thing found themselves back in Zimbabwe the next day. You will not get far. This white farmer will call his police friends. They will arrest you before you get anywhere and deport you back to Zimbabwe,' said Mazvita.

'So you're saying we are in some sort of a prison?' I asked.

'On the surface, yes. The farmer will do everything he can to keep you here. The only way others have successfully escaped is by doing it secretly in the dead of night. There are a lot of gossips on this farm. Those who have planned an escape have kept it to themselves. It's partly why so many people are still here. They didn't know about the plan, so they couldn't escape with others,' said Mazvita.

'I thought he was a very nice man,' said Gertrude, sounding downtrodden.

Mazvita turned away from the pan to face us, one hand on her hip, the other waving a spatula in our direction.

'He is the cruellest white man I have ever met,' she said, anger seeping through all of her violent gestures. 'There was a young Zimbabwean boy working on the farm he was said to be sodomizing. That boy disappeared just after some of the workers had threatened to report him to the police. People say he killed that poor little boy,' said Mazvita.

Visions of the white man taking Sheila into his large house flashed across my mind. I could hardly breathe.

'Is he gay?' I blurted out.

'He is. He targets most of the young boys at this farm,' replied Mazvita.

'So what should I do to get out of this place safely? How did others leave this awful place?' said Gertrude.

'There is a driver who comes to pick up vegetables on Tuesday and Friday mornings. He is sympathetic to the workers here. I will talk to him first. I think he will be able to help you.'

'What about you, Nyasha? Where are you going from here?' asked Gertrude.

'I don't know anyone in this country,' I answered.

The reality set in as I spoke. Where else could we go? Who would be willing to help Sheila and me? After what happened at the river, I didn't want to venture outside on my own with Sheila. I felt tears stinging my eyes as I spoke.

'It looks as if I am going to keep Mazvita company for some time,' I replied.

Gertrude shook her head rapidly. She walked to my side and, grabbing my hand, looking at Mazvita, and said, 'You and Sheila can come with me. You can both come with me. My brother is a very nice guy. He will be more than happy to help you, I'm sure of it.'

I smiled in appreciation to Gertrude and her kindness. But

my thoughts, as always, turned to Peter. *I pray and hope that Gertrude's brother will help me track down Peter. I need to find my husband as quickly as I can.*

'Really? He would take me in? But you hardly know me,' Mazvita exclaimed.

'You are one of us,' Gertrude said, after a pause. 'We need to stick together and help each other in this foreign land. I know my brother will feel the same.'

Her face lit up. 'At last! I am finally going to leave this farm!' said the excited Mazvita.

'Just persuade that driver to help us,' said Gertrude.

'Oh my God! Thank you so much! At last my prayers have been answered. Thank you, Gertrude! Thank you!' She grasped Gertrude's other hand and shook it rapidly.

'You're welcome,' replied Gertrude, a small smile tugging at the corners of her mouth.

I wasn't sure how I felt. Mazvita's reaction and excitement revealed how desperately she wanted to get away from this farm. And from what she had told us, it was clear it was a bad place to be. But would leaving the farm be any better?

'Is the pay good at this farm?' I asked.

'We work from five in the morning to ten at night. We get thirty rands per day,' replied Mazvita.

'We might as well all be slaves for that kind of salary. How can the farmer get away with such blatant robbery?' said Gertrude.

'That's not right. That must be against South African labour laws,' I echoed.

'Who is going to listen to an illegal immigrant? Before you

finish reporting the farmer, you will be back in Zimbabwe. This farmer is well connected,' replied Mazvita.

I turned back to the vegetables, finishing the preparations for the meal. My head was spinning while my eyes were brimming with tears. I had most of the information I wanted about the farm. I was glad about Gertrude's offer. I was just praying for the driver to agree to help us. How could our lives change so rapidly? What if we do not escape? What would happen to Sheila and me? If we were able to escape and were able to establish a life, to earn money, perhaps I could send for Peter - if he was still alive.

We continued with the meal. The electric stove was very fast; we were finished in thirty minutes. We took the food to the others and ate. As Gertrude and I cleaned up, Mazvita prepared a place for us to sleep. Sleep could not come fast enough.

At five o'clock in the morning, Zivai came and started banging our door.

'Everyone in the fields now!' he screamed.

We ignored him. We had just slept a few hours and, since we had arrived in the middle of the night, figured we would have a day to rest.

The door was swung open, banging against the wall.

'Hey, didn't you hear what I just said!' he screamed, pulling our blankets off us.

'We can't work, we've just barely arrived and have had no chance to sleep,' Zvanyadza protested, angry, trying to take her blanket back from Zivai.

'I am sorry, my sister. I am not the one who creates the rules at this place. I'm just doing my job. The boss wants to see everyone, including all of you, working in ten minutes time,' said Zivai.

We had no choice. We got up and started preparing to go out to work.

'What about the kids?' I asked.

'The kids are not allowed in the fields. They will have to stay here. There are other kids here they can play with,' replied Zivai.

We left Sheila and Esther behind and followed him to the fields. Mr. Volek was waiting for us. The others had already started working, including all the men we had come with but Titus. The work was hard and painful. No one was allowed to talk or eat during working hours.

Mr. Volek and Zivai walked around making sure the rules were being obeyed and that everyone was working. We spent the majority of the day bent over working, praying Mr. Volek would feel we were working hard enough. Within the first ten minutes of us working, we saw what he could do when he approached a man working slowly, clearly in pain, whether from an illness or previous cruelty, I wasn't sure. The cruelty Mr. Volek showed to the man was extreme. He beat him severely. The man could hardly stand. But Mr. Volek expected him to continue working. I was now beginning to understand why Mazvita cried with excitement at the prospect of leaving the farm. I felt sorry for the woman. To imagine that she had endured this hard life for three long years was shocking. I didn't think I would be able to do it for more than one week. *We have to do all we can to escape*, I thought.

The day went by quickly.

'It's now noon! It's lunchtime! I want everyone back here by exactly one. If you are late, money will be deducted from your pay,' shouted Mr. Volek.

With one hour to cook and eat, we knew we had to move quickly. No wonder Mazvita's fridge was full of chicken livers. The farm workers had to make meals that were quick and easy.

All the workers ran at full speed to their kitchens. We cooked, ate and were back in the fields five minutes early.

We continued like that for the next two days. On the third day after work, Mazvita pulled Gertrude and me aside to give us the good news.

'I've talked to the driver,' she whispered.

'That's good. What did he say?' I asked.

'He has been asked to do a pickup tomorrow and he is willing to help us. Tomorrow may be our only shot,' said Mazvita.

'So what did you say to him?' asked Gertrude, looking around to make sure no one could hear.

'I told him we are ready. I can't wait to leave this place.'

'Excellent. So where do we meet him, then?' I asked, anxious to be away from this place as well.

'We'll have to slip out at three in the morning. I know the road he uses to come here. We'll have to keep walking until he comes along, to avoid suspicion,' said Mazvita.

'Till morning, then,' whispered Gertrude.

'Please don't tell anyone about this,' said Mazvita.

We nodded our heads in agreement and joined the others. I was excited, but one thought continued to make me uneasy - Esther. How could I leave her? Sheila and Esther were now inseparable. And I had made a promise to Chiwoniso that I would help take care of her.

The girls were now like real sisters. Trying to separate them would be a cruelty. I thought of taking Esther with us, but I knew Brighton would hate me for the rest of his life if I took her from him. She was the only connection he had left to Chiwoniso. I didn't know what to do. I would hate to leave Esther behind. Brighton was not part of the arrangement Mazvita had made with the driver, so I couldn't have him join us.

Esther was now my daughter. The only way to save her from the farm was to talk to Brighton and ask him if he would allow me to take Esther with me. But I had promised Mazvita I would tell no one about our escape. Any discussion with Brighton would be an act of betrayal to Mazvita and Gertrude. I wasn't sure what to do.

I looked at the two girls as they played and giggled together. My heart ached with pain at the thought of Esther's life without Sheila and Sheila's life without Esther. She didn't deserve this, especially after losing her mother so soon. These girls couldn't lose another person in their life. I couldn't leave her behind.

I made up my mind to speak to Brighton. I took him for a walk, far from everyone else, and told him my plan.

He shook his head as soon as I suggested taking Esther. 'I can't let you take her! She is all I have now.'

'I understand, but Brighton, you must think of Esther. Not only is she like a daughter to me, but her and Sheila are inseparable. To separate them after such pain in both of their lives would be cruel,' I said.

'I know, and I am very appreciative of the role you have played since Chiwoniso's death, but I believe you also can understand my position. She needs to be with her father. I need to take care of her and protect her.' He turned and started walking away.

'Please!' I begged, grabbing his arm.

'I'm sorry,' replied Brighton.

I knew I couldn't change Brighton's mind.

'All the best then,' I said, holding back my tears as I thought of leaving Esther.

'Till we meet again then, Nyasha,' said Brighton as he turned and grasped my hand. 'I pray that God will be with you.'

'Thank you,' I said and began walking away.

'Nyasha!' he said and I stopped. 'Thank you for your support through everything. I don't know how Esther and I would have made it without you.'

I looked at him, nodded my head and walked away. I didn't want to cry in front of him. Getting Sheila out without Esther would be extremely difficult. The girls slept together. If Esther happened to wake up while we were leaving, it would complicate everything. She would want to know where we were going and she would want to come with us.

Evening came, but I couldn't sleep. Esther's situation was still disturbing me. Brighton had tried to make Esther come and sleep with him in his room, but she had refused. She had made it clear that wherever Sheila slept she would sleep also. I gazed at her the whole night as she slept peacefully, not knowing how different the next day would be. I wondered how she was going to react in the morning once she discovered that we had run away. She considered me her mother and Sheila her sister. I prayed that she would not feel the same pain she had felt the night she had lost her natural mother.

I found myself crying. It was too painful for me to bear. In the dark, in the middle of the night, tears trickled down my cheeks.

'I'm sorry, Chiwoniso. I have failed you. I have failed to keep my promise. Please forgive me,' I whispered, hoping Chiwoniso would understand my situation. I spent the whole night staring at my two little girls and wiping away my tears as they continued trickling down my cheeks.

I heard a slight tap on the window and knew that Mazvita had come. I didn't have a watch, so I was shocked that it was already three in the morning. Time had gone by too quickly. I woke up Gertrude, took a blanket, and fastened the sleeping Sheila on my back. I was glad she didn't wake up, otherwise she would have made some noise and possibly awoken Esther.

In a few minutes, we had taken all our belongings and were ready to leave. I stood there for a while looking at Esther sleeping peacefully. I had never felt so guilty. In some ways, this was the most selfish thing I had ever done, choosing my well-being at the expense of an innocent six-year-old girl. I felt horrible. I was now thinking of calling the whole escape plan off to make sure the two girls were always together and looked after properly.

Then I began thinking I should just ignore Brighton and take Esther with me. *But what if something bad happens to Esther on our way? How could I look at Brighton again? He would kill me.*

Gertrude, on seeing the internal dilemma I was going through, took my hand and pulled me out of the room.

The impatient Mazvita frowned when she saw my face full of tears. She waved at us to follow her. We tiptoed through the fields till we got to a nearby dusty road. We walked a long way down it, hoping to see the lorry driver early, but it wasn't so, so we just kept walking on.

After about two hours of walking, we finally saw a red lorry coming from the direction we were walking towards.

'That's Thokozani. That's the driver,' said Mazvita and sighed. She was as tired as I was.

'I was really starting to get worried. I wasn't sure what we would do if he hadn't turned up,' I said.

'I was getting worried, too,' said Mazvita.

The driver came to where we were and stopped.

'Morning, ladies,' said Thokozani.

'Morning,' we all greeted him.

'You keep walking. I will go and pick the items up at the farm and then I will come back and pick you up,' said Thokozani.

'Thank you, we will see you when you come back,' said Mazvita.

'Mum, where are we going?' asked Sheila, now awakened by the noise of the lorry. 'Where is Esther?'

I pretended I could not hear her. We smiled and waved goodbye to the driver as he drove off. We felt relieved knowing our help had arrived. I was going to a place where I could start my life again, where I would hopefully have the resources to find my husband. *Don't worry Peter, wherever you are. Everything is going to be all right. I will do all that I can to make sure you join us here.*

'Mum! Where is Esther?' asked Sheila, tears beginning to fill her eyes.

We all looked at each other, not knowing how to answer the little girl.

'We left Esther at the farm, dear. We are going to pick up something and will come back. You will be with your friend soon,' replied Gertrude.

I was pleased with Gertrude's response, as it did calm Sheila down a bit, but she still looked unhappy that we had left her best friend behind. Esther was now part of her life and she didn't want to spend a day without her.

CHAPTER 13

We continued to walk, but this time we were dragging our feet, always looking backwards to check if the red lorry was approaching. It didn't take long for our wish to be fulfilled. The lorry finally arrived.

'Hop in, ladies!' shouted the smiling Thokozani after he had pulled in front of us. We were finally on our way to freedom. *I hope to get settled quickly so I can make plans for Peter to join me.*

'Finally,' Thokozani said, grinning at Mazvita as we climbed into the lorry. 'I was beginning to think you were going to die at the farm.'

'You wanted me to die at the cruel hands of Mr. Volek, I know,' said Mazvita.

Thokozani jerked his head around, staring at Mazvita in shock. 'What makes you think that?'

'For three years, you came and left and never bothered to help me.'

'You never asked. And what did I do when you did ask? What do you call what I am doing now?' said Thokozani.

Mazvita was clearly annoyed. Thokozani looked confused. I tried to change the subject.

'We want to thank you for your help, Thokozani,' I said.

'You are welcome. At least you are not unappreciative like your friend,' said Thokozani, sighing.

'Come on Thokozani, you know me better than that,' said Mazvita, her expression softening. 'You know I didn't have anywhere else to go otherwise I would have escaped long time ago.'

'You ladies should have seen the look on Mr. Volek's face,' said Thokozani.

'Was he upset?' asked Mazvita.

'What would you expect? Mazvita was one of his most precious workers. The situation was made worse by a little girl who got on his nerves by constantly crying,' said Thokozani.

'Was she in the fields? Mr. Volek has never allowed kids anywhere near the fields,' said Mazvita.

'They tried everything to get her off the fields, but they failed. She kept coming back crying. She was screaming that she wanted Sheila. She wanted to be by her father's side.'

That hit me hard. I broke down and started crying. Sheila started crying as well. It was my fault. I had abandoned her and now she was hurting. I felt so bad. I wished I had taken her with me.

Thokozani looked at Sheila and me, confusion crossing his face again.

'Oh, did I just say something I wasn't supposed to say?'

'Yes. The little girl you just mentioned,' said Gertrude.

'I am so sorry. Is she her daughter?' asked Thokozani.

'Sort of,' said Mazvita.

'What is that supposed to mean?' asked Thokozani.

'That little girl's mum was her best friend and she had

promised to look after her, but the father would not allow us to take her, so we had no choice but to leave her behind,' said Gertrude.

'So where is her real mother?' asked Thokozani.

'She is dead,' replied Gertrude.

'Oh, poor little girl,' said Thokozani.

'Nyasha, please don't cry. There was nothing you could have done,' said Mazvita.

'I feel so guilty!' I replied, sobbing.

'Don't put all the blame on yourself, Nyasha. You did all you could. Brighton will never let anything bad happen to that little girl,' said Mazvita.

We drove for a while and, after some time, I managed to calm myself and Sheila down.

'Can I please borrow your phone?' said Gertrude.

'I hope you don't want to call your boyfriend in Zimbabwe' said Thokozani. 'The cost of that phone call is pretty high.'

'Of course not. I want to call my brother in Mpumalanga,' said Gertrude.

'Oh, you have a brother here? Where exactly in Mpumalanga is he?' asked Thokozani.

'I don't know exactly where,' replied Gertrude.

'That's fine, here you go,' said Thokozani as he passed the mobile phone to her. She reached into her handbag and took out a small torn notebook. She punched some digits from the notebook into the phone, placed the handset to her ear and waited.

'Hello, can I speak to Muzhindu?' said Gertrude.

We all kept quiet to give her time to talk to her brother. Thokozani lowered the volume of his radio.

'Oh! My brother! It's me, Gertrude,' she said.

We all looked at her as she smiled and giggled. I was eager to hear what her brother was saying. I wished she had put the phone on speaker.

'I'm fine, I'm fine. Yes, I am here now.' she paused for a while. 'It's a long story, my brother. I will tell you when I get there,' she said and paused as she listened to what her brother was saying. 'We are three adults and one little girl. We are all women,' she said looking at us, smiling.

Obviously, the brother wanted to know who these strangers were, since she was bringing us to his home. I knew his accepting us was important. Our future depended on his assistance, since we had no relatives or friends in the area. Silently, I was praying that he would help us.

'Thank you so much, thank you brother. So how do we get to your place?' she asked with a big grin on her face.

Her reaction showed that her brother was willing to help us, hopefully until we got settled. I was relieved.

'That's fine, we will wait for you in Johannesburg then,' said Gertrude and she hung up.

'What did he say?' asked Mazvita. She was anxious for the details, as was I.

'He says he will accommodate the three of us and he is coming to pick us up in Johannesburg,' replied Gertrude.

'Oh, how nice of him. May God bless him,' I said.

'Where in Johannesburg is he going to meet you?' asked Thokozani.

'He said by the coach station,' said Gertrude.

'OK, that's not too far; I will drop you there.'

'Thank you,' said Gertrude.

He took back the phone and turned up the volume of his car radio. After an advertisement finished playing, a song by Lucky Dube came on. The song was Peter's favourite. He had bought the CD from Harare from the time he had worked there. Since we didn't have a radio, he would take the CD with him to the shops in town and beg the shop owner to play it for him as he relaxed with his friends.

I remembered passing by the shops a couple of days before we had been taken. I saw him dancing to the song. I missed him so much. God had blessed me with a kind and loving husband. All the years we had been together he had never raised his hand to beat me. We had arguments many times, but when he was upset, he would just go with his music to the shops and come back later in a jovial mood. *I am here now Peter, we are safe. I will make sure you come as well and we will be that happy family again. This time you will not dance to your favourite song on your own, but I will dance with you. I can't wait for you to come. I long to be in your arms once again. I long to see you bring Sheila her favourite fruits every night.*

Since I had not slept the previous night, I was struggling to keep my eyes open, regardless of the excitement I felt, knowing I was going to get help. I fell asleep.

'Nyasha! Nyasha! Nyasha!' I heard Mazvita calling as Sheila shook me, trying to wake me up. I opened my eyes slowly.

'What?' I asked, yawning.

'We have arrived,' said Gertrude.

'Wow, that was quick,' I said.

'Mum, you always think the trip is quick, it's just because you fell asleep,' said Sheila, giggling.

'Sir, can I please borrow your phone again? I want to tell my brother that we have arrived,' said Gertrude.

'Here you go,' said Thokozani as he gave her the phone.

She punched in the number again and waited.

'Yes, brother, it's me again. We are in Johannesburg now,' said Gertrude, smiling.

Johannesburg was full of people, more than I had seen in any city near my village. I wondered how this big city coped with so many people around. While I had been to Harare many times before, the crowds were nothing compared to this.

'OK brother, thank you. We'll ask around. We'll find it,' said Gertrude. She gave the phone back to Thokozani.

'What does he want you to find?' asked Thokozani.

'He wants us to wait for him at the taxi rank for taxis that go to Ermelo,' replied Gertrude.

'I'm not exactly sure where the taxi ranks are, but you should be able to ask anyone on the street and they can direct you. I wish you all the best,' said Thokozani.

'Thank you very much. May God richly bless you,' Gertrude responded. We all thanked him.

'If things don't go your way, just go back to the farm. Mr. Volek will be more than happy to see you again!' said Thokozani, laughing.

'Never! I would rather go back to Zimbabwe,' said Mazvita.

Still laughing, Thokozani waved as he began driving away. 'Take care, ladies.'

'Wait! Before you go, give me your phone number,

Thokozani. You never know what will happen in life. We might need your help again,' said Mazvita.

We waited as he wrote his phone number on a piece of paper. He gave it to Mazvita, waved goodbye, and drove off.

We struggled to find the taxi rank, as many people we came across couldn't speak English and we couldn't speak Zulu. Mazvita had learned a bit of Afrikaans at the farm, but it wasn't too helpful. We eventually met a Zimbabwean who was kind enough to take us to the taxi rank we were seeking. We then waited for Muzhindu.

After thirty minutes, he arrived. Gertrude introduced us to him. Seeing that we were hungry, he took us out for barbecue. The food was fantastic. I had never consumed so much meat at once in my life. Sheila was thrilled and hardly knew what to do with all of the food in front of her. This was a totally different life from the one we had experienced in our village and while getting to South Africa. I was also pleased to see it was a different South Africa to the one we had been introduced to when we crossed the border.

'This is nice,' Mazvita said, patting her stomach. 'Is this how everyone lives here?'

'This is the treat we usually give everybody who comes here for the first time,' replied Muzhindu. 'It is a popular restaurant here, and the food is good.'

'Well, thank you; we feel honoured to be welcomed like this,' said Mazvita.

'Especially when you have spent the whole year eating chicken livers!' said Gertrude, laughing.

I can't wait to give Peter the same treat. When he comes I will take him to this same restaurant. Considering how much he loves meat, I know he'll be thrilled to eat here.

We couldn't finish the meat; it was too much. Gertrude packed some up to take back and we headed for the taxi rank again. Muzhindu paid for our taxi fares. It took us about an hour and a half to get to Ermelo, a small town within the Mpumalanga province.

He was renting a three-room house in Wessolton, a small suburb of Ermelo. He used one room as the bedroom with his wife Rachel. The other he used as an office and the third was a combined kitchen and sitting room. I was surprised to see many computers and printers filling his office. It made me wonder what exactly he did for a living.

His wife, Rachel, was very welcoming as well. She prepared some hot water for us to bath in and gave us some of her clothes to change into. She took Sheila out to the shops and bought her two dresses and a pair of shoes while I was bathing. *Does this mean our nightmare is finally over?* I thought. This is what I had dreamed South Africa would be like. Now I had the opportunity to mould our lives into a future that would be beyond our imagination - a future of milk and honey, of empowerment, of opportunities and of peace and harmony, things Mugabe's government had failed to give us.

Muzhindu and his wife explained to us how the new South Africa had transformed their lives. They had started with nothing and were now making a good amount of money, living a decent life compared to the way they had been living in Zimbabwe. They had bought themselves a very nice car, which would have taken them over twenty years to save money to buy if they had stayed in Zimbabwe. Muzhindu had not brought it with him to Johannesburg since he had yet to get a driver's licence, but they both frequently used it locally. With the amount of money they had saved, they were planning to go back to Zimbabwe and buy a big house as soon as things had calmed down. Hearing of their success was sweet music to my ears.

I began imagining what my life could be like. I imagined my new life with Peter and Sheila in our own beautiful house in the high-density suburbs of Harare. How lovely it would be to have Peter drive our brand new car to church on a Sunday morning. That lovely feeling quickly turned into sorrow as the pictures of the last time I saw Peter played back in my mind.

Remembering the shaky voice of Adamson as he asked Fadzi if my husband was dead, I was slowly growing depressed. I needed to think about something different, and quickly. Lamenting over what I could never have was making it difficult to remember the miracle of being saved from the farm.

I tried to concentrate on the South African gospel music video which was being watched by everyone as they had migrated over to the couch to relax, but the scenes of that painful night kept flashing before me. My thoughts shifted from Peter to myself as I saw Adamson and Fadzi pulling my legs wide apart. My past was refusing to fade away. It just kept haunting me. I needed to fight my thoughts and move on with my new life, a life full of hope.

I tried to focus on my daughter, the only person who made each day of my life worth living. I looked at her as she licked an ice cream which Muzhindu had given her. She would lick and then look at her beautiful dress and shoes, clearly excited to be out of the clothes she had worn since we fled. She looked beautiful. I was really proud of her. She had been through so much over the last couple weeks and yet she remained so strong. She saw that I was looking at her and grinned shyly. I smiled back.

My thoughts drifted to my other 'daughter', Esther, whom I had abandoned at the farm. I imagined her sitting next to Sheila in a new dress and with her own ice cream in her hand. I remembered how Thokozani had described the last time he had seen her in the fields, crying. My vision got blurry as tears filled my eyes.

'Nyasha! Your drink!' shouted Mazvita.

'Oh, I'm sorry,' I said as I straightened the tilted cup of tea that had begun to spill.

I had almost forgotten that I was holding something in my hand. Muzhindu saw that my eyes were full of tears.

'Are you OK?' asked Muzhindu.

'Yes, I am fine,' I replied, fighting the tears that were about to fall. 'Can you please excuse me?' I stood up, went to the toilet, and wept.

In the evening, the three of us slept in the sitting room along with Sheila. I had difficulty falling asleep. I couldn't help but wonder at how I was going to contact Peter. I didn't have anyone's phone number in Nyamutumbu. This was becoming more frustrating than I had imagined.

Muzhindu and his wife took turns doing some work in their home-based office. They said that they had a big order that had to be completed the next day. I wondered what kind of business they ran. But it was none of my business; I was just grateful for the help they had offered us.

CHAPTER 14

In the morning, someone banging on the door at about five in the morning awoke us. We got up and saw Muzhindu let four men and two women into the house.

'Did you finish the stuff I texted you about last night?' asked one of the men as they walked in.

'I did. Come in,' replied Muzhindu as he went into his office.

'*Makadiiko?*' the visitors greeted us, asking us how we were.

'*Tiripo makadiiwo!*' we replied – very well. We enquired in turn whether they too were fine.

'*Tiripo,*' they replied - fine.

They were all from our country, but they were so nicely dressed that they could easily have passed for South Africans. Muzhindu came back holding three cases of about 100 DVDs each.

'Is that all you have?' asked one of the ladies.

'No. I have more to bring out,' replied Muzhindu as he went back into his office. He came back holding three more DVD cases, went back again and brought out three more. All in all, there were 900 DVDs. When I looked more closely at them, I understood. Gertrude's brother made pirated music and DVDs. I was surprised, mainly at the fact that he could get away with it without getting into trouble. But it was none of my business. Like many Zimbabweans who had come to this country, he was trying to survive.

My mind drifted back to how I was going to track down Peter. *How am I going to do this? Maybe he is no longer in Nyamutumbu. Maybe he is no longer alive. No, he can't be dead. Who can I call in Nyamutumbu?* I thought as I looked at the visitors doing business with Muzhindu.

The women and men went through the DVDs, selecting the ones they wanted. The visitors each took 100. At six rands per DVD, he was able to collect 3,600 rands that morning. We had just seen a few of his customers and we didn't know how many more people he was supplying to every month. I couldn't help but wonder just how much money he was making.

'So, ladies, this is how I make my money,' said Muzhindu after his customers had left.

'They took a lot of DVDs. Will they be able to sell all of them?' asked Mazvita.

'They selected the ones they know are in demand. Don't be surprised to see them coming for more tomorrow morning,' replied Muzhindu.

'It must be a big business then,' I said.

'It is. We used to go out and sell them ourselves and it was very good, but now we are suppliers to many different sellers. We don't have the time to go out and do the sales ourselves.'

'How much will they be selling each DVD for?' asked Gertrude.

'Twenty rands each.'

'My goodness, that profit is huge,' said Mazvita.

'It is. Most of them have bought themselves cars from this. You could see from their clothes that they have some money,' said Muzhindu.

'If I was to meet them in the streets, I would have thought they worked in offices at some big company,' said Gertrude.

All this time, I was calculating how much I would need to be able to start that kind of a business myself. To start with 100 DVDs, it would mean I needed 600 rands as capital, but I didn't have any money on me. I couldn't even afford to buy Sheila some sweets. I began wondering if I should have stayed on the farm for a bit. I could probably have managed to save a bit of money.

'My wife will take you out with some DVDs today to train you how to work in this business, if you would like,' said Muzhindu.

'But brother, we don't have any money at the moment,' said Gertrude.

'Don't worry about that. When you start selling, you can pay me back what you owe bit by bit,' said Muzhindu.

The sense of relief I felt was great, but fear also crept in. *This is illegal. What if I get arrested? Who will look after Sheila? Without any travelling documents, they would definitely deport me. What should I do? But how else will I make money? I'll have to take the risk for now until I can find something else.*

'Thank you, brother,' said Gertrude.

I was glad. I couldn't believe that by the evening I would have some rands in my pocket. Eventually I would be able to buy my daughter all the things she wanted. I would then save some money and send it back home to Peter, so that he could follow and join us. The more I thought about it, the more excited I was getting.

I now understood part of Muzhindu's generosity towards us. Obviously, he wanted to help his sister and her friends. But we were also adding to the number of people he supplied to, increasing his monthly income. I couldn't blame him for that. He still took us in, which not many people would have done. He had paid for our transportation from Johannesburg, bought Sheila some new clothes, accommodated us, fed us, and now he was giving us a job, a business we could run ourselves.

We bathed, had our breakfast and started making preparations for our first day out as saleswomen. I wasn't feeling comfortable in the dress that Rachel had given me so I asked her if I could have another one. She took me into her bedroom to try a few of the dresses she was no longer wearing. On the left of her wardrobe was a clothes wire rack where a wet towel and some pants were hanging. Right next to the towel were red panties, exactly like the ones I had been wearing before we were attacked - the same panties I had taken off as I planned to give Peter the sexual experience of a lifetime.

My thoughts returned to the plans running through my head before Zanu PF's militia arrived. I thought of the way I had wanted to make love to him that night. I thought of how he would have reacted to finding me without panties. *We can still do it when he comes. We can pick up from where we left off the day he arrives. But when is that going to happen? When is he going to come? Oh, I long to make love to him. God, help me track him down.*

Then, all of a sudden, my thoughts jumped to the moment when the bald man had told Fadzi to take my panties off. I could see the grinning faces of the militia men looking at my privates after they had found out I wasn't wearing any panties. *Would Peter ever want to make love to me again after being raped? Would he view me as his wife or a prostitute?* My thoughts were beginning to depress me. I needed to focus on the new task which was before me and raise some money for Peter to come.

Rachel asked a neighbour she was friendly with to watch Sheila. The neighbour had a little girl of her age, which worked perfectly. They helped us to sort the DVDs and distribute them evenly among ourselves so that each had the DVDs that were on demand. After double-checking that we had all we needed, we left.

As we walked away from their house down the street, Rachel began explaining exactly how the business worked.

'We don't sell in our area because if the police find out, they will have an easy time finding where we live and they'll come and seize all our computers. Instead we take a taxi and start in an area where people don't know us as well.'

'So what do we do if we are caught by the police?' I asked.

'The police in this country are very corrupt. You just bribe them and they will let you go. But always make sure you don't let them know where you live or who your supplier is,' replied Rachel.

Hearing this made me nervous. The police were my biggest worry. I didn't want to risk getting myself deported back to the place I had run away from. I would have to be extra careful. We got in a taxi and Rachel told the driver where to go. After driving a few kilometres, we got off.

'This place is called Thusi. I had a lot of customers here

when I used to go out and sell. I will try and introduce you to them all so that you have a client base when you are on your own,' said Rachel.

'Thank you,' I said.

'But we can't speak Zulu. How are we going to be able to communicate with them?' asked Gertrude.

'You will have to learn it, fast. It's to your advantage, but there are a lot of them who do understand English as well,' replied Rachel.

We followed her as she led us to meet some of her old customers. The language barrier was going to be a big problem for me. I wasn't good with languages. I remembered when I had tried to learn Ndebele and found it very difficult. I had given it up in the end. I wished I had continued, because Zulu and Ndebele have many similar words.

'The rest of you wait here. Nyasha, come with me,' said Rachel as she entered the gate of the first customer. '*Koko! Koko! Koko!*' she shouted as we stood outside the front door.

'*Ngena!* [Come in!],' a female voice shouted from inside the house. Rachel waved at me to follow and we entered the house.

'Oh my God! Where have you been?' asked the female customer with excitement as soon as she saw Rachel.

'I've been travelling,' Rachel lied. 'It's been a long time. It's good to see you.'

'You too. It has been a long time since I last saw you,' said the woman.

'I know,' said Rachel. 'This is my sister Nyasha. I came with her from Zimbabwe.'

'Nice to meet you,' said the woman, smiling.

'Nice to meet you, too,' I said.

'Your sister is one of my best friends, but she just disappeared without telling me she was travelling' she said to me. 'Can you imagine? Is that what a friend should do?'

'That's not nice at all,' I said. 'I hope she won't do that again.'

I could see that Rachel couldn't remember her customer's name. If she had known it, she would have said it to me. What was important, however, was that we got the money we had come for.

'I hope you have brought me my favourite Nigerian movies. Oh, please sit down,' she said, gesturing towards her chairs.

'Yes, we have a few of them. My sister will bring you more next time,' she replied as we sat down. 'Nyasha, please take out your DVD wallet.'

As I took the DVD wallet out, her two children appeared.

'Do you have the latest DJ Fish?' asked one of them.

'Yes,' replied Rachel.

'How about Rebecca Malope's new live DVD?' asked the other kid.

'We don't have that particular DVD, but we have the CD instead,' replied Rachel.

I took out the wallet and gave it to them. They screamed with excitement as they sifted through it. I watched as they argued over which ones they should take. I felt at home and was very comfortable watching the children interact. Hopefully all the customers would be the same.

'We want to take seven, but I only have enough for five now. You can come back and collect the balance next Friday,' said the woman.

'That is fine, but remember it will be my sister who will come to collect the cash,' said Rachel.

'That's fine; I hope she won't get lost,' said the lady as she took 100 rands from her purse and gave them to me.

'I won't get lost. What time should I come?' I asked.

'Any time. I'm always here,' replied the customer. 'If I have to go somewhere, I will leave the money with my kids.'

'No problem,' I said with a big smile on my face as I examined the first rands coming into my hands.

'Can you please bring Rebecca Malope's DVD when you come next week?' asked one of the kids.

'And some Kwaito music,' said the other.

I nodded my head in agreement. 'Thank you,' I said as I put the money in my handbag.

'Say, *Ngiyabonga*,' said the lady.

'*Ngi-ya-bo-nga*,' I managed to say.

'That's it. *Ngiyabonga* means thank you. You must start learning Zulu now,' said the lady customer.

'We have to go now. *Ngiyabonga kakhulu* [Thank you very much],' said Rachel.

'Bye! *Hamba khale*. [Have a nice journey],' said the woman.

I came out with a huge grin on my face. I was delighted. In a very short period of time, I was 100 rands richer. I knew I would have to put extra effort into learning the language, but it was a big opportunity for me to make a lot of money.

We continued street by street, from one house to the next, taking turns with Rachel going into different houses. At most houses we got cash and in others we would give the DVDs on credit.

Step by step, we were building our client base through Rachel's contacts. By the time we got back home, I had made 300 rands in cash and was looking forward to collecting the rest I had given out on credit.

CHAPTER 15

Within two days, Mazvita was looking for a small room and was able to move out, as she had saved a little from her farm salary. She was very excited and full of energy. This work was much easier and better than the work she had done on the farm.

I bought Sheila and myself some new clothes and shoes. It was great to have more than the clothes on our backs to change into. My next big purchase was a mobile phone. Not only was it important to get customers' phone numbers and give them my number so that they could call me if they needed something, but I desperately wanted to get information about my husband. My one problem, however, was that there was no one I knew in Nyamutumbu village who had a mobile phone.

Two days later, I was able to pay Muzhindu all that I owed him and started looking for a room to rent. I managed to get a very cheap room in Dhlamini, a small shanty town a few kilometres from Muzhindu's place. I moved out with Sheila on May 13 2008, but I came back every day early in the morning to leave Sheila and get more DVDs.

Rachel loved my daughter very much, and Sheila loved going over there. She never gave them any trouble and she had already made a few friends around the neighbourhood whom she played with daily. It amazed me how quickly she had picked up Zulu. In the evenings after my day's work, I would collect her and we would go back to our small room in Dhlamini.

As days went by, my Zulu was improving and, surprisingly, I had made a few friends around our area who were helping me with the language. After I ran out of ideas on tracking down my husband, I talked to Muzhindu, who suggested using the internet. He asked if I had any relatives in Harare and I thought of my aunt, who ran a small store. Thankfully, she sold some of her products by advertising in one of the local newspapers, which we found online. We got her number and gave her a call. I waited impatiently as my aunt's phone rang.

'Hello,' a female voice answered the phone.

'Can I please speak to Auntie Emma?' I said.

'Who am I talking to?' asked the female voice.

'My name is Nyasha Gapa from Murehwa,' I replied.

'Ah, Nyasha! Oh my God! How did you find my number? How are you?' said Aunt Emma.

'I am fine, Auntie. It's been a long time! How are you?' I asked.

'How are Sheila and Peter?' asked Auntie Emma. 'But where are you calling from? This looks like an international phone number.'

'I am calling from South Africa. Sheila is fine, but I don't know about Peter. We had to run away. *Chakabvondoka* [political unrest]', I said. 'I am very worried about my husband.'

'Oh I am sorry to hear that, dear. Don't say too much on the phone, you never know who is listening.'

'I need you to do me a favour, Auntie,' I said.

'What do you want me to do?' she asked.

'I want you to go and check on Peter for me. I need him to come here as soon as possible.'

'That's hard. Strangers are not that welcome in rural areas these days. It sounds like the political unrest has got even more intense since you left. Going to your village would be dangerous. But I will be going to Mutoko in a few days and on my way back, I can pass by your mother's place. They at least know me there,' said Aunt Emma.

'I would appreciate that. Thanks, Auntie. I know my mum will have some information,' I said.

'When I am at your mother's place, I will call you to let you know I am there. Then you can call back and talk to her.'

'That sounds great. This is my number. Just call me when you get there, I will be waiting. Thank you very much,' I said.

'You are welcome,' she replied.

'I have to go now. Please say hello to everyone for me.'

'I will do that. Stay blessed, bye,' she said and hung up.

I was glad that I had finally talked to someone at home. The idea of speaking to my mother made me happy. I wished Aunt Emma had been going to Mutoko that day. My mother would definitely send someone to look for Peter and from there, if the news was good, we could begin making arrangements for him to follow. Sheila would be over the moon to see her father again. It would be nice to surprise her, but I would keep it a secret until he came.

The following day, May 17, I woke up excited and full of hope. After speaking with my aunt, I knew I would be hearing about Peter soon. As usual, I took Sheila to Muzhindu's place and proceeded to another small, highly-populated suburb called Sun City where a few customers had asked me to come and collect what they owed me. I decided to do some selling first before meeting my other customers.

'*Koko*,' I said, knocking as I got to the first house.

'*Ngena*! (Come in)' a female voice responded.

I entered a small two-bedroom house. There were four men sitting around a table drinking some type of alcohol and one woman who was cooking something in a corner of the room.

'*Sawubona*!' I greeted them.

'*Yebo*! [Yes!]' the lady replied.

'*Ngiya thengisa ama* DVD [I am selling DVDs]' I said

'Ithi *ngiwabone* [Let me see them],' said one of the men.

I moved close and gave him my CD wallet.

'*Hlala phansi* [Sit down],' said the man.

'*Ngiyabonga* [Thanks],' I replied.

The lady left what she was doing and came to look at the DVDs. One of the men said something in Zulu, which was too deep for me to understand. I didn't respond because I wasn't sure if he was talking to me or to his mates, but he sounded upset.

'*Ukhuluma isiZulu na* [Do you speak Zulu]?' the man barked at me.

'I'm sorry. *Ngiyafunda isiZulu* [I am learning Zulu],' I said.

'*Uyakhuluma isilungu na* [Do you speak English]?'

'*Yebo.*'

'Right, what I'm explaining to my friends here is that I am a musician and we are failing to make any money because of people like you,' said the man.

'I am sorry, sir. We are just trying to survive. Things are hard,' I said, looking at him in confusion.

He didn't look angry, but mischievous. I wasn't sure what he was trying to accomplish with this conversation.

'What about us? How do you expect us to survive then?' asked the man, folding his arms across his chest.

I didn't reply. I didn't want to provoke him more. I could see he was up to something. I wished I could just grab my DVD wallet from them and run away.

No one knew where I was and the people I was conversing with could do whatever they wanted to me without anyone knowing. The memory of the schoolhouse came flooding into my mind. There were four men and one woman. With their combined strength, they could get away with anything. I hadn't quite realised the dangers the business could bring until that moment. My hands began shaking. I could feel small beads of sweat forming on my forehead. I began looking around, making sure I could quickly escape.

'*Amakwirikwiri* [Selfish foreigners]!' cursed the lady as she went back to what she was doing. I jumped when I heard her speak. I didn't understand what she said, but I could tell she was angry. The man said something that I also didn't understand.

'*Biza amaphoyisa* [Call the police]!' barked the other man.

'Did you hear that, foreigner? We are going to call the police!' the first man shouted in delight.

I jumped up. 'Please, please, don't call the police,' I begged.

'What are you waiting for, then? Get out now!' barked one of them.

I could see there was no way they were going to give me my DVD wallet back. I was too nervous to try and get it back. I didn't want the men to hurt me or hold me until the police came. I quickly walked out, leaving my DVDs behind.

'*Hamba khale* [Have a nice journey]!' barked the woman as I opened the door to leave. I didn't reply. I was upset and shocked that the woman had even bothered to say goodbye. I had just lost 100 DVDs, which were worth 2,000 rands. I had now lost the 600 rands I had used to buy them with. Since selling the DVDs was illegal, I couldn't report my case to the police. Still upset, I went to see Muzhindu and let him know what had happened.

'I know the house you are talking about. They saw that you were a woman and that there was nothing you could do to them. They outnumbered you and knew they could take advantage of you. They are not musicians; they are just a bunch of thugs,' said Muzhindu.

I looked down, holding back tears. While it was a relief to know the police would likely not be called, I could hardly bear the amount of money I had lost just by visiting that one house.

Rachel came over to me, wrapping a comforting arm around my shoulders.

'I'm sorry, Nyasha, but you have to understand that these kinds of things are part of the business. Sometimes you make a lot and sometimes you lose all your stock. There are good days and bad days. You just hit a bad one.'

'There was one time when the police came to where we used to live. They took all our computers and printers; everything we needed to make a living. That's when we moved to this place. We had to start all over,' said Muzhindu.

'What does *Amakwirikwiri* mean?' I asked.

'Is that what they called you?' asked Rachel.

'Yes, they called me that; they sounded very angry when they said it.'

Muzhindu shook his head. 'I hope the attacks will not move to this area.'

'What attacks?' I asked, concerned.

'Last week there were some foreigners who were attacked and killed in Cape Town. The South Africans who killed them were singing a song about *Amakwirikwiris*, meaning that all foreigners must go back to their countries,' said Muzhindu.

My stomach clenched. What had happened to us in Zimbabwe was because of our political affiliation. Could something similar happen to us again simply because we weren't from South Africa? I was overwhelmed by the thought. Regardless, I gave a simple reply.

'That's bad,' I said.

'Some Zimbabweans were actually among the dead' said Rachel.

I said a quick goodbye to Rachel and Muzhindu, leaving to pick up Sheila and absorb what they just told me. Not only was I demoralised by what had just happened to me, losing both my inventory and my money, but also by the attacks on foreigners. Would we ever be safe?

I decided to take a break for the rest of the day and spend time with Sheila. I had been working hard for so long and hadn't had quality time with my daughter. Now seemed like a perfect day to spend more time with her. We went out to eat.

Sheila was thrilled to be in a restaurant. I was thrilled to see my daughter so happy. I wished Peter and Esther were around, too. I just hoped it would last.

CHAPTER 16

I woke up early in the morning of May 18 2008 with even more determination to achieve my goals. I wasn't going to allow what had happened to me the previous day to prevent me from making money for Sheila and Peter. I hoped I would soon be in touch with my husband and money would be needed for his travel documents and expenses. My job was a big opportunity for us to transform our lives and I wanted to take advantage of it as much as possible. I also needed to save some money to help Esther and Brighton get away from the farm and start somewhere new.

I took my bath, made our breakfast and took Sheila to Muzhindu's place. Mazvita and Gertrude were there waiting for me. They wanted a description of the house where I had been robbed so that they could avoid going there in the future.

'Good to see you, Nyasha. I thought you wouldn't be coming today,' said Rachel.

'Good morning. Why did you think I wouldn't come?' I asked.

'I thought you would still be scared by what happened yesterday.'

'Oh, that is behind me now. I have gone through scarier things than that before,' I said as I looked at Muzhindu, who had just walked in.

'Ladies, I'm going to have to give you some more advice before you go out today,' said Muzhindu as he sat down.

'OK,' said Gertrude as she packed some DVDs in her wallet.

'When you enter a customer's house and you see some suspicious people inside, don't say you are selling DVDs. Change your story. You can pretend you're looking for someone,' said Muzhindu.

'It's also best to get other things to sell as well, like brooms or something similar, so you can just say you are selling them when you come across suspicious people,' added Rachel.

'Also, get a small notebook and write down all the customers you give DVDS on credit. Not all customers are trustworthy,' said Muzhindu.

'All in all, don't be afraid. We have been in this trade for years and have seen a lot. It is rare to be in danger while out selling,' added Rachel.

They gave us more advice and, after they had finished, it was time to go out again. I selected my DVDs, thanked them for their advice, and left with Gertrude and Mazvita, each taking her own direction, since we had collections in different places.

I went to Thusi and started selling from there. After about five hours I was tired and hungry, so I decided to rest and get myself something to eat. I bought a drink and a packet of chips. I sat down, relaxing, as I enjoyed my small lunch. I began thinking about Peter and about all of the ways we could make a life for ourselves here. We could be happy, I thought.

I was startled out of my thoughts by the ringing of my

mobile phone. I took it out of my handbag and looked at the number. It was Muzhindu. I was surprised. He had never called me while I was working before.

I decided not to answer it. I needed to get back to work and wanted to get as much time in as possible. *Maybe there was something wrong with Sheila,* I thought. *But why didn't Rachel call me instead? Wasn't Muzhindu out working?*

After a few minutes, the phone rang again. I figured that if he was calling a second time, it must be about something important.

'Hello,' I said softly.

'Hi Nyasha. Where are you?' asked Muzhindu.

'I am in Thusi. Is everything OK?' I asked.

'Everything is fine. Can you come back now please?' said Muzhindu.

'Why now? Can't I just finish what I am doing first, and then come home in the evening like normal?'

'No! You have to come now,' persisted Muzhindu.

I didn't like the tone of his voice. Something must be wrong.

'You're scaring me, Muzhindu. Is there something wrong with my baby?' I asked.

'Sheila is fine. She is playing with her friends outside. Just come now please,' begged Muzhindu.

'OK, if you insist,' I said.

'I will see you soon then.'

'OK,' I said and ended the call.

I was worried. I wondered what was so urgent that Muzhindu couldn't tell me on the phone. There had to be something wrong with Sheila. Why else would he call? I knew I couldn't blame him for not telling me what was going on over the phone. I would have been afraid to tell someone sad news over the phone. You never know what they might do when they receive bad news.

I had lost my appetite. I left the food, to the surprise of the strangers walking past me, and went to find a taxi. I got a taxi, got off close to where Muzhindu lived, and walked as fast as I could to Muzhindu's house.

I saw my little girl with her friends. She saw me and smiled. She was clearly happy that I had come back early. She must have thought I was going to take her out to eat again.

'Mummy! Mummy! Mummy!' Sheila screamed and ran towards me as I approached Muzhindu's house.

She came and jumped into my arms. I hugged her and stood there for a while, feeling her small body wrapped around mine. I was relieved. My daughter was fine. So what had really gone wrong? What else could be happening to make Muzhindu ask me to come back that urgently?

Maybe they had heard some news about Peter. I almost fainted at the thought, especially considering it could have been bad news, with the state I had left him in. I was confused. Maybe it was something to do with Esther?

I gathered some courage; there was no point in tormenting myself when I was just a yard away from the information I was so eager to get.

I sighed and walked towards the door. I knocked at the door and it was Muzhindu who opened it for me. Inside were Mazvita, Rachel, Gertrude and one of the men who had come to get DVDs on our first morning in Ermelo.

They all looked sad and serious, glued to Muzhindu's small screen television. They were listening to the news and were so focused that they didn't notice when I walked into the room.

'*Maswera sei?*' I said, enquiring if they had had a pleasant day so far.

'*Taswera bho*, Nyasha,' they greeted me back, but they didn't take their eyes away from the television.

I looked at Muzhindu, expecting him to begin explaining why he had disturbed my workday. Sheila was fine; what else could possibly be wrong? I hoped they had not called me to simply waste my time watching television, because I didn't have time for that. I had goals and needs that could only be sorted out with money. He didn't say anything. He too was too focused on the television to tell me what was going on.

'Can you tell me why you called me back? I need to get back out as soon as possible,' I said.

'I'm afraid you won't be going anywhere today, my friend,' said Mazvita.

'Why?' I asked.

'The xenophobic attacks are spreading. Some Zimbabweans have been killed in Johannesburg and we are afraid the attacks might start spilling to this area at any time,' said Muzhindu.

'They know that most people who go around selling things are foreigners, so that will make us their first targets,' said Muzhindu's friend.

'Why aren't the police doing anything about this?' I asked, getting angry.

How could the land I thought was my salvation turn into another hell?

'They don't want us here. I imagine many foreigners will flee and go back to their countries after this. I wouldn't be surprised to hear that the attackers were being paid by the government to do it,' said Rachel in disgust.

I was speechless. I sat down and joined them in watching the news updates to find out what was happening in other cities. The video clips of what was happening were painful and heartbreaking. People were being ruthlessly beaten and tortured; some had even been burnt alive. They were accusing us foreigners of taking their jobs.

The news was a strong reminder of what had happened to Peter and me. I couldn't handle it. I didn't want to go through something so awful again. I had seen enough.

I decided to go home and rest. I said goodbye, promising Rachel, Muzhindu, Mazvita, and Gertrude that I would keep a low profile until the violence blew over. I went outside to look for my little girl. A group of children, Sheila among them, was now sitting outside the house of Muzhindu's neighbour. Five kids sat around Sheila as she narrated something to them. I wondered what she was telling them. It must be the African tales I used to tell her every night, I thought.

I was impressed by how quickly she had learned Zulu. Spending hours and hours playing with children who spoke the language had helped immensely. I was eager to hear what my daughter was telling them, so I slowly tiptoed towards where they were sitting.

They didn't see me, as they were all listening attentively. In broken Zulu and sometimes mixing in Shona, she told them her story.

'About three very big crocodiles swam towards the dog. One swam right for my uncle and I closed my eyes,' said Sheila, covering her eyes.

'Did the crocodiles eat him?' asked one of the kids, engaged.

'No. Edwin, Brighton, Tafara and Wellington jumped in and beat the crocodile with branches,' Sheila exclaimed, grabbing a stick and jumping up. She then hit the rock she was sitting on with the stick, reenacting the adventure. 'He was hurt pretty bad. But the others got the crocodile off him and pulled him away from the crocodiles. We then hurried into the jungle so the crocodiles couldn't find us again.'

'What about the dogs? Why didn't they bite the crocodiles?' asked another kid.

'I heard the dog crying after the crocodiles came to them. I think the crocodiles ate the dog,' said Sheila.

'I thought the crocodiles would be afraid of the dogs,' said another kid, looking confused.

'Sheila! It's time to go home!' I shouted, disappointing the children listening to the story.

I could see by the expressions on her friends' faces that they were unhappy with me taking Sheila before she had finished telling them the full story.

'Oh, Mum! Can I just play a little bit more?' said Sheila.

'No, my darling. You can come back and play tomorrow,' I replied. 'Come on, let's go.'

She scowled as she slowly got up. She dragged her feet as she walked towards me, looking very upset.

'Bye, Sheila!' said one of the kids.

She didn't reply, but just waved at them. She was very upset. We found a taxi and got in. I tried asking her about her day, but she didn't say a word until we got home. I started preparing dinner. After I had finished the cooking and set the table, we sat down to eat.

'I am sorry that I took you away when you were still having fun with your friends,' I apologized, trying to engage her in a conversation

'You always do that, Mum. Why?' she asked, still upset.

'Sometimes, we have to do things we don't want to do. Tonight, we needed to go home, even though you wanted to stay with your friends. I know it is hard to do sometimes. I said I am sorry. Are you not going to forgive me?' I said.

'OK, I forgive you. I don't want to go to hell, Mum,' she replied.

I laughed, impressed that she had not forgotten the things we had taught her, but also that she would say that out loud. I was the one who had taught her that people who don't forgive would be burnt by a fiery furnace in hell. I just never expected her to say it as a fact.

'So do you always think about the things that happened to us when we were coming here?' I asked, remembering what she was telling her friends.

'Not always,' she replied.

'But sometimes,' I said.

'Yes,' she paused for a moment. 'And sometimes I dream of it, too.'

'Really?'

'Yes,' she said as she nodded her head. She looked slightly nervous.

'What kind of dreams? Do you still remember some of the dreams?' I asked, worried by that revelation, hoping they were not like my nightmares.

'I dreamt of Auntie Chiwoniso before…and of Uncle Titus crossing the river,' she said.

'Do you remember what happened in the dreams?' I asked.

She paused for a while, thinking. I looked at her. She amazed me with the way she talked at times. Sometimes she talked like a grown-up girl who you'd never think was five years old. She was growing up very fast and in a few months' time she would be turning six.

'One time, it was on my birthday and Daddy had arranged a party for me. All my friends had come. Esther was there, too. We had so much fun until Auntie Chiwoniso came. She was holding some chocolates and a doll. She was moving very, very slowly.

'I was very happy, saying that Auntie Chiwoniso had brought me some sweets and a doll for my birthday. Everyone stopped what they were doing and stared at her. When we all stopped to look at her, she stopped to look at us. She yelled my name and asked me to come to her. I looked at you and you said I should go to her.'

'I walked towards her slowly. But when I got closer, she began changing into an ugly, scary beast. I turned around to try and run back, but two men came and grabbed me; they started pulling me towards her. I screamed for help but no one came. No one saved me. Everyone was laughing. I was scared and they were laughing. You were laughing, too. Then I woke up,' said Sheila, looking down. She was clearly upset just remembering the dream.

'Well, that is a very weird dream. What about the one about Uncle Titus?' I asked. She paused for a while, thinking again.

'I don't really remember it all,' she said. 'You know the river that we took baths in, in Nyamutumbu?'

'The Shanhuwe river,' I said.

'Yes, that one. Me, you, daddy and Uncle Titus were in a boat in that river. Something happened and the boat started sinking. That's all I can remember, Mum,' she said. I was heartbroken she was having such nightmares. I was so focused on the nightmares I was battling, I didn't even think about hers.

'It was just a dream, darling. I hope you know that. Those things will never happen to you. We'll never cross that river again,' I said.

'OK,' she shrugged, continuing to eat her food. She clearly had her doubts.

CHAPTER 17

We kept quiet for a while, concentrating on the food and thinking over what was said. I thought of all the dreams she had told me about. I remembered what my pastor had told us. According to him, it was not a good thing to dream about dead people. But how could we do otherwise?

'I don't want you telling people everything we went through when we were coming here,' I said.

'I was telling my friends. They are not just people,' she said.

'I still don't want you telling anyone what we went through on our way here, regardless of whether or not they're your friends. We need to keep it a secret. Do you think you can do that?' I asked.

'But why? My friends like my stories.'

'Well, some people don't like those kinds of stories. They could get mad. Will you promise not to tell those stories to your friends anymore?'

'Yes, Mum,' replied Sheila.

We continued to eat.

'Do you want more soup, darling?' I asked.

She shook her head, looking at me.

'When are we going to see Esther? I miss her so much.'

I sighed and placed my hand on her cheek.

'I just want us to raise more money. Then we will go and see her,' I said.

'But what if I don't see her again?' said Sheila.

'You don't have to say that. You will see her again,' I said, patting her cheek.

'You lied, though.'

I was shocked to hear her say such a thing. 'What do you mean? When did I lie to you?'

'You said that Daddy was going to meet us here, but he hasn't come. I don't really think we are ever going to go back to the farm again, or see Daddy,' she said.

'I promise you, darling, you will see your daddy again and you will see Esther again,' I said.

'I just miss them, Mum. I miss them so much,' she said tearfully. I stood up and hugged her.

'It's OK, it's OK,' I said as I consoled my sobbing daughter. 'Mummy just needs to work a bit harder, and then we will send your daddy and your best friend some money so that they can come here.'

The ringing of my mobile phone interrupted our embrace. I reached into my handbag, but by the time I took my phone out it had stopped ringing. I went to the missed calls section on my phone to check who had just called me. Sheila looked at me, surprised by the huge grin on my face.

'Who is it, Mum?' she asked.

'It's Auntie Emma from Harare,' I replied.

It didn't excite her much because she couldn't remember her - the last time Peter and I had visited Auntie Emma she had still been very young. But I was over the moon. This meant that she was now at my mother's place, as she had promised that she was going to call me when she got there. The thought of hearing my mother's voice was thrilling, but knowing that I might get information on the whereabouts of my husband made me even more excited.

'I must call her back. Let's go and buy a top-up voucher, darling,' I said as I looked for some money in my handbag.

We rushed out to buy the voucher. We came back and as I was busy punching the digits to top up my phone, I heard some people singing outside. The sound was far away, but it seemed to be moving towards our house.

'Is there a funeral somewhere close, Mum?' asked Sheila, looking confused as she looked out the window.

'No, darling. People in this country don't do funerals like we do at home,' I replied as I finished entering the numbers.

The sound was very close to our house now. Feeling anxious, I moved over by Sheila to look out the window. I couldn't see anyone yet, but the singers were definitely getting closer.

'I'm scared, Mum,' said Sheila, grabbing my hand.

'Don't be scared, darling, it's just people passing by,' I said, shaking slightly as I spoke.

'I remember the people who took you and Daddy away. They came to our home singing. What if they take you away? Then who is going to look after me, Mum?' she asked.

I knelt down and looked intensely into Sheila's eyes.

'No one will take me anywhere, Sheila. I will be here to take care of you always. Don't be afraid of anything, OK?' I said, trying to hide my own fear, which had gripped me.

I couldn't bear the thought of Sheila being alone. I had to know about Peter. As Sheila turned back to the window, watching for the singers, I picked up my mobile phone and dialed my aunt's number.

'Hello,' Aunt Emma answered the phone.

'Auntie, it's me, Nyasha. How are you?' I said.

'I am fine. I am at your mum's place. I had just gone out to get something from my car. Let me run back and give the phone to your mum, hold on,' she said.

I waited, eagerly anticipating hearing my mother's sweet, frail voice. Then Sheila yelled. I gasped. I could hear the singing people. They were right outside our house.

'Foreigners must go
To their countries they must go
They are taking all our jobs
They are raping our women and robbing us
To their countries they must go.'

They sang at the top of their voices. My body went numb with fear once I understood what they were singing. Everyone who lived around our house knew I was from Zimbabwe. That was no secret in our neighbourhood. And after Sheila told our story to so many children, it was no secret to anyone nearby. The song was meant for me. I tiptoed to the door, opening it slowly, and peered out to see what was going on. There were over thirty people with sticks, steel pipes, and golf clubs singing; some had their faces covered.

'Let the foreigner come out.
If she doesn't come out we will burn her inside
Amakwirikwiri come out
Bloody foreigners come out.'

They sang the words with no look of remorse. Rather, a look of savage excitement.

Three men came towards my door. I quickly shut it, throwing the locks in place. Running to Sheila, I scooped her up in my arms and held her close as they started banging on my door. I heard a noise, a quiet talking, and realised I still had Auntie Emma on the phone. I started crying. I put the phone up to my ear. I heard my mum asking Auntie Emma if it was really me because all she could hear were people crying.

'Mum! It's me, Nyasha,' I sobbed, as I could hear footsteps going round our small house.

'Nyasha, why are you crying? What's wrong? What's going on there?' asked my worried mum.

'Mum, I love you so much. If anything happens to me, I want you to know that I love you,' I sobbed.

'Why are you talking like that, Nyasha? What's happening to you?' asked my mum. She began crying as well.

'If you see Peter, tell him that I love him so much. I love him with all my heart,' I sobbed.

I could hear my mother and aunt crying, but I had to focus. I couldn't let my fear overtake me. Sheila clung to my legs as I tried to figure out what the mob was doing outside. I smelled petrol and realised what they were planning. I stood in shock, dropping the phone. I stepped on the phone and hit the loudspeaker button as I rushed to the window. I could hear my mum crying.

'Oh, Nyasha, my daughter! What is this now? Oh God, please save my daughter from whatever it is! Whatever it is, God. I know nothing is too difficult for you. You took Daniel out of a fiery furnace. Hear my cry and take my daughter out of this situation.'

Sheila heard her grandmother's words and started crying harder, as did I.

'Nyasha! Nyasha! Nyasha! Can you hear me, Nyasha! Tell us what's going on!' I heard my aunt beg.

The two men whose footsteps I had heard earlier were continuing to walk around the house, pouring petrol around the perimeter. Through the holes of our door I could see men and women surrounding our house, singing jubilantly. I didn't know what to do.

If I were to run out of the house, they would butcher me to death. I had seen on television what they had done to the victims in Johannesburg. Going outside wasn't an option. I was now trapped with no one to help and nowhere to run. My daughter was trapped as well. I took my sobbing and shaking daughter into my arms, knelt down on the floor and prayed.

'Lord, if it is your will to end my life in this way, I accept, but please save my daughter, for she doesn't deserve to die like this. Forgive me all my sins.' I then paused, thinking of the people outside. 'And forgive these people, for they don't know what they are doing.'

And then it began. Smoke seeped in through the window. Moments later, we could see the fire. We heard the crackling.

We could feel the heat. We both screamed as the flames slowly took over. Sheila clung to me even harder. We both sobbed. I could hear my mum and aunt wailing after they heard our screams. The heat was quickly getting to be unbearable and I could see the house slowly crumbling. I needed to do something quickly, something to save Sheila. *It's only me they want*, I thought. *They don't want a child. If Sheila were to get out, they wouldn't, they couldn't, harm her. She is just a child. They wouldn't harm a child.*

'Sheila,' I said, releasing her hold and turning her around to face me. 'I want you to run out. I want you to keep running. When you see the police, tell them to take you to Muzhindu's place,' I said, trying to stop the tears from rolling down my face.

'What about you?' asked my daughter, trying desperately to speak through her sobs.

'Don't worry about me; I will be fine. You'll see me at Muzhindu's. Remember, I love you and will always love you.'

'I love you too, Mum,' she replied, hugging me tightly.

I didn't want to let her go. I couldn't bear the thought of her losing her mother, of her never seeing Peter or me again. I couldn't bear the thought of never feeling her small body against mine, never feeling that small, tender, beautiful heart beat against my chest.

I pulled her back, wiping her tears from her cheeks. I gave her a smile. I saw a faint smile beginning to form on her lips. I stood up, holding her hand and hurrying her towards the door.

'Go now, Sheila,' I said as I opened the door.

She hesitated.

CHAPTER SEVENTEEN

'Run, my daughter. Run!'

Sheila hesitated a moment and then sprinted out of the door. The flames luckily hadn't reached it yet, but they were quickly approaching. I closed the door and moved to the window. I watched as my daughter ran away from the burning house. I felt my spirits lift as I saw her pass some of the mob members. They did nothing to her and simply let her pass. But then, from behind the group, a tall dark man ran towards her holding a golf club. I whimpered, praying he was running for the house and not her.

I knew I was silly to hope she would be spared as soon as that man appeared. The man reached Sheila in seconds, swung the golf club around, and hit Sheila on the head. I heard my daughter scream as she flew into the air.

I let out a shriek. 'No!' I couldn't believe what I was seeing.

I hopelessly watched as her frail, small body slowly tumbled to the ground. Repeatedly, he hit my daughter with the stick as she helplessly lay down. The mob rejoiced and celebrated as the man walked back to them. My daughter wasn't moving. There was no way she could have survived such a brutal attack. It was my fault. I shouldn't have let her out.

'My daughter!' I screamed, banging on the window. 'Oh God, why? I have killed my daughter! I have killed my daughter!' I screamed.

I sobbed, hardly able to breathe. I heard a voice screaming. It was my mother, still on speakerphone.

'Nyasha! Nyasha! Nyasha! What has happened to Sheila?' I heard my sobbing mother ask.

I crawled to where the phone was. The fire had reached the

166

inside of the house. The walls were burning. I moved slowly, trying to avoid the sting and heat of the flames.

'I am sorry, Mum. I won't be seeing you again. I am so sorry. Know that I love you,' I sobbed.

'What's going on Nyasha? Tell us what's going on?' my sobbing mum asked, but I didn't want to answer. I hung up the phone and looked up. I could see the fire was burning through the roof. It would fall at any moment. But I didn't care. My daughter was dead. I was dead.

I helplessly watched as the burning roof fell over me. Then everything went black.

CHAPTER 18

I heard a beep. Then another beep. *I'm dead,* I thought. *Why is something beeping, in Heaven?* I listened closely, trying to understand my new surroundings. My eyes were heavy, so I kept them closed for a while. The beeping sound continued. I heard some footsteps and various voices. The sounds became clearer. People were mumbling something, but I couldn't quite make it out. I then heard someone crying. *Why would someone cry in Heaven?* Then it hit. The pain. My body felt like it was on fire. My head was thudding in agony. *Heaven? This must be Hell,* I thought.

I slowly tried to lift my heavy eyelids. As soon as the light hit them, I snapped my eyelids shut, my eyes aching with pain.

'Nurse! Nurse! She is awake! She is awake!' I heard a female voice shouting with excitement.

I realised at that moment that I wasn't dead. I was alive. *How did I survive the fire?* I thought. I wanted to ask whoever I had heard calling the nurse about my daughter. I moved my lips, but I had no strength to utter a single word.

'She moved her lips! She is trying to say something!' screamed the female voice again.

Someone came. It must have been the nurse. I felt hands pressing different points of my body. I was jumping with pain every time I felt pressure from the touch.

'It looks like she is out of the coma. She is responding now,' said the female nurse. 'I will let the doctor know.'

So I had been in a coma. How long had I been out? *Where is Sheila? Where is my darling daughter? Where is Peter?*

I kept trying to open my eyes. After some minutes of trying, I managed to open them slightly. I could make out some blurry figures around the hospital bed. I could see Muzhindu, Rachel, Mazvita, Gertrude, and a man who was holding something looking like a Bible. That must be the Pastor, I thought. They each gave me a huge grin as I slowly moved my eyes, looking at each one of them.

'Where is... Sheila? Where...is...my...daughter?' I whispered, struggling for air.

'What is she saying?' asked Muzhindu.

'I couldn't quite understand her, but I think she is asking about her daughter,' said Gertrude.

'Just rest for now, Nyasha. Everything is well. Everything is going to be fine,' said Rachel.

I could see that they were trying to avoid my question. I closed my eyes, exhausted by the small amount of energy I had to use to simply ask my question. But at the same time, I desperately wanted to see my daughter. I had to know if she was all right.

Hour by hour, I was slowly gaining my strength and memory. The pictures of what had happened before waking up in the hospital were slowly coming together. I remembered the flame that engulfed my small home. I was sure I had been burned, probably badly, as I had no memory of leaving the burning house. Burns would explain the bandages covering almost every part of my body.

By the next day, I had greatly improved. I was able to speak clearly, stay awake, and focus on what was going on around me. But the pain was still severe. In the afternoon, Muzhindu, Rachel, Gertrude and Mazvita came to see me. They explained what had happened. I had been in a coma for six days.

'God is good. Very soon you will be fully recovered and you will be coming back home,' said Gertrude.

'Where is Sheila?' I asked.

No one replied. They all just looked at each other. I remembered Sheila being hit with a golf club, but I hoped, rather than believed, that she had survived and was in the same hospital with me. The look they carried on their faces said it all. I started crying. I didn't want to believe that I had lost my beautiful, innocent girl. She should have survived and I should have died.

'We are so sorry, Nyasha,' said Mazvita.

The memory of what had happened came back to me. I told her to leave the house. I told her to escape. I naïvely thought she would be spared by the mob. Instead, they had killed her. No, they hadn't killed her - I had.

'I killed my daughter. I killed her!' I wept.

'What do you mean?' Rachel inquired.

Between sobs, I explained what had happened.

'The house was burning. I knew there was no escape for me. If I left the house, they would have killed me on the spot. I thought I was done for. But I thought the mob would have spared a child, a little girl.'

I cried harder, having a hard time getting the words out.

'I told Sheila to run. I told her to run past the mob and get help. When she left, I thought she would be all right. Most of the people she passed did nothing. But one man came forward. He killed her.'

Everyone was silent. Mazvita and Gertrude each held my hands, comforting me as I cried.

'It's not your fault, Nyasha. There was nothing you could have done,' said Muzhindu.

'No, Muzhindu. I could have had her stay with me.'

'That would have been just as big a risk, Nyasha,' Gertrude said. 'You don't know if she would have survived the fire. Her little body would have been engulfed in the flames. Or, if she had received the same blow to the head you had received, she would probably have died.'

'Where is her body? I want to see her,' I said.

'She is in the mortuary, they won't allow you to see her, not now,' said Muzhindu.

I had never felt so guilty. My daughter was dead because of my decision, because of what I told her to do. I remembered the dreams she had told me about before that terrible tragedy. She had already been scared. She was so scared something would happen to her, to me. I had assured her she would be safe. Instead, she had been beaten to death. I would never forgive myself. Never. I should have died, not Sheila.

Later, the doctor came to examine me. I could barely focus on what they were saying. My thoughts were with my daughter. I kept expecting her to bounce into the room, hugging me, kissing me, telling me about her day. But she never came. And the longer I didn't see her, the more I felt empty inside. *How am I going to tell my husband? Would he ever forgive me for my decision that cost our daughter her life?*

After some effort, I was finally able to focus on what the doctor was telling me.

'The good news is that you are responding well to medication. With any luck, you'll be able to go home in a few weeks. You sustained third degree burns across almost your entire body, so we had to do some skin grafts. We will continue to monitor the wounds to make sure they are healing properly. Worst case scenario, we might have to do more skin grafts, depending on how your skin heals,' he explained.

'Thank you,' I replied. After making some notes on my file, the doctor moved on to the other patients.

For days, I continued with the treatments, steadily gaining my strength. After a few more days I was able to move around, which included going to the restroom. I received the shock of my life when I looked into the mirror. I couldn't recognise myself. My face was totally disfigured. I was scary looking, ugly, and a completely different person. I looked like a monster. My face was full of blisters. My entire face was swollen and my skin was peeling off. It was featureless. It was white in some areas and black in others. I had no hair, no lips and no eyelashes. I screamed and ran away from my own reflection. The nurses had to calm me down and get me back to my room. I was so ugly that people would run for their lives when they saw me. *If Peter is alive, how will he ever want me back? I look hideous. I'll never be beautiful again. But I don't care how I look. I must see him. I miss him so much.*

After a few weeks, I was discharged from the hospital. On the day I got out, June 12, I asked Muzhindu to take me to my house. He refused at first, saying it wasn't a good idea, considering the events that had occurred at the place. But I persisted. I had to visit the home where my daughter was killed. My wounds were not completely healed, so I covered my head with a veil to keep away the flies that constantly hovered around my face.

He drove me to the house and parked in front of what was left of the place I had once called home. It looked as if no one had attempted to touch anything from the day we had been attacked.

I was the first to get out of the car, followed by Muzhindu, Rachel, Gertrude and Mazvita, who all came for support. I stood in the place where I had seen my daughter crumple helplessly to the ground after she had been struck by the golf stick. It was as if I had pushed the replay button. I could hear my mother sobbing on the phone. I could see the frightened face of my daughter. Everything had happened so fast on that fateful day that I hadn't noticed the details. I could see everything clearly now. I could see that she was frightened, but there had been an unusual twinkle in her eyes. *Why, I wondered? Why was her soul full of joy? Did she see what was in front of her? Was she happy about the place she was going to?*

'It's terrible what happened here. I guess you must be the relatives?' asked Khanyisile, my neighbour who had come over to where we stood.

'Yes,' replied Muzhindu.

'I'm terribly sorry about what you guys have gone through.

I hear the kid and her mum didn't make it,' said Khanyisile.

'Only the kid' said Gertrude.

'Oh! So where is the mother now?' she asked.

There was silence. No one seemed to know how to respond to the woman.

'My daughter didn't deserve this, I will not rest until justice is done,' I tearfully said, breaking the silence.

'Nyasha! I am so sorry, I did not recognise you. I'm very sorry about all this. When I saw the mob surrounding your house and singing, I called the police, but they didn't arrive in time,' she explained.

'It's OK,' I replied.

I had lied. It wasn't OK. *I* wasn't OK. I was angry. Angry with all my neighbours. I knew one of them must have told the mob I was a foreigner, leading them to my house. They were as guilty as the man who had murdered my daughter. I wanted her to leave and I knew how to scare her off.

'It's a crazy world we live in nowadays,' she said as she moved slowly towards me.

I turned round to face her and raised the veil, revealing my wounds.

'Yeah, you are right. There are too many crazy people around,' I said as I looked at her.

'Jesus!' she said as she came face to face with my monstrous face.

'Excuse me' I said, eyeing her with my eyelash-less eyes.

'I have left a pot full of meat on the stove. I need to check it. Please, if you need anything, don't hesitate to give me a shout,' she said as she backed away from me.

'Thank you,' chipped in Mazvita.

Yes, go away. Go to your home, now you have news to give to your friends when we have left. You gossips, you good-for-nothing women, you family breakers. Tell all your mates how ugly you have made me now.

'Can we please go now?' asked Gertrude.

Gertrude pulled me out of my thoughts. I focused on Sheila. *The only place I want to go to now is where my daughter is. I want to find out if she is well and happy. I just want my daughter. I want my family back. That's all I want now.*

My last moments with Sheila flashed back again. I saw our last hug, the last time she said she loved me and the last time I looked into her eyes. I looked at her closely in my mind, but this time it wasn't her eyes which stared at me. It was Peter's eyes. I knew my daughter had her father's eyes, but this time it was as if they had been plucked out of his face and forced into Sheila's. The eyes were tearful and sorrowful. It was as if Peter knew what had happened and was asking me why I had let her out. Why didn't I protect her? Why did I kill her? *Does he really know that Sheila is dead? Does he blame me for her death?*

'I'm sorry Peter. I'm so sorry. All I wanted was to protect her and I thought I was doing what was right. I thought they would spare a little innocent girl!' I wailed.

When Gertrude embraced me I realized I was shaking terribly. I sobbed for a while in her arms.

When I let go of her, I looked to my right. A small distance from where we stood lay one of Sheila's shoes. I walked towards it and picked it up. This was one of the shoes Rachel had bought her the day we arrived at Muzhindu's place. I remembered the first time she had put them on, licking an ice cream and frequently glancing at her feet. She was happy and never stopped smiling. *Is she as happy now as she was then? Is she smiling now? Does she miss me? Does she miss her friends? Does she miss Peter?*

The pain I felt was unbearable. My feet became weak and I felt like I was about to faint. I staggered and went down on my knees. Gertrude and Mazvita rushed over and picked me up.

'Get me out of this place now. Get me out of this place, please. Please take me home,' I sobbed.

With Gertrude and Mazvita by my side, they helped me walk back to the car. I looked around and saw many of my neighbours looking through their windows. I wondered what was going through their minds. I was sure they knew the person who had murdered my daughter. *Can't they see the grief I am going through? Do they have any conscience? If they were really sorry for me, they would have told the police who killed Sheila. Why can't life be simple and normal for me? Oh God why? Why can't my family be back to what it was before? How much more turmoil do I have to bear?* I glanced at the murder scene for the last time as Muzhindu put his car in gear and drove off.

CHAPTER 19

I continued visiting the hospital regularly for my treatment and checkups. I forced myself to get through each day. My face was taking different forms and shapes everyday as the wounds began to heal. It was strange to look at my face in the mirror every day and see a different reflection from the one I had seen the previous day.

'How do I look today?' I asked Rachel, who was helping me prepare for my doctor's appointment.

'The swelling has gone down a bit,' she replied.

I had moved back into their place since my house had been destroyed by the fire. I was very grateful for all they were doing for me.

'I have a different look every day. My face is always changing. Maybe I should change my name, too. What do you think of 'Many Faces'?' I asked, smiling as I thought of the new name.

'Many might work out well as a first name but I've never heard anyone with Faces as a surname,' she replied, smiling back at me.

I could see relief written on her face. I reckoned this was because of my smile. I couldn't remember when I had last smiled. They had tried all they could to cheer me up, but nothing ever worked. Today I was in a different mood. I had changed my focus. Now that Sheila was gone, Peter was all I had left. Through all the pain I felt, both physically and emotionally, I knew I had to get back to him. I had to become strong.

I moved over to the mirror, eager to see how I looked when I smiled. I looked even more monstrous, so I turned away to face the still smiling Rachel.

'I will be the first person to have Faces as a second name,' I said.

'Miss Faces. No, it doesn't sound right. Unless you want to be a rap star of some sort,' she said giggling.

I glanced at the clock and saw we were running late, so we took all my medical documents and rushed to the hospital.

After one week, and with my permission, Muzhindu started making preparations for Sheila's burial. I needed to update my relatives back home on what had happened, but all my belongings and my aunt's phone number had been destroyed in the fire. Muzhindu decided to track down my aunt again. Once more he got her number from the website she used to advertise her products and called. I waited impatiently as Muzhindu waited for the phone to be answered on the other side.

'Hello, is this Auntie Emma?' said Muzhindu.

My aunt must have asked who it was, as Muzhindu gave a brief introduction of himself.

'Hold on for Nyasha,' said Muzhindu as he passed the phone to me.

'Hello,' I said, taking the phone from Muzhindu.

'Who am I speaking to?' asked my aunt, sounding confused.

'It's me, Auntie. Nyasha' I replied.

'Nyasha? Nyasha who?'

'Nyasha Gapa.'

She gasped. 'Is this some kind of a joke? Please don't waste my time. I've got better things to do!' she said.

'It's not a joke, Auntie Emma. The last time I talked to you was when Sheila and I were attacked. I know you thought I was killed, but by God's grace I survived. How is my mum?' I asked.

'Oh my God! We all thought you were killed! God is great! Hearing your voice brings me so much happiness,' said Auntie Emma.

'I am happy to hear your voice, too, Auntie,' I said.

'Your mum will be over the moon when she hears this. Ever since your accident, she hasn't been the same,' she said.

'So when can you go back to Murehwa?' I asked.

'I can't, I'm flying to the United Kingdom tomorrow morning' she said. 'But I will try to send someone down there to give your mother the news.'

'Did you hear anything about my husband?' I asked.

'They did send someone to your husband's place the last day I was there, but I couldn't wait for the person to come back because of work commitments,' she said. 'So how is Sheila? She wasn't hurt, was she?'

I felt my throat tighten up. I didn't know how to give her the news. How would I tell Sheila's family, who loved her dearly, that she was dead? I sighed and kept quiet for a while.

'Hello, Nyasha? Are you still there?' asked my aunt.

'Sheila... Sheila didn't make it, Auntie,' I forced myself to say as I began to cry.

'What do you mean, Nyasha?' she asked.

'They killed my little girl, Auntie. Sheila is dead,' I said, the tears beginning to flow freely.

She kept quiet for a while. Her joy and excitement quickly turned into sorrow as she heard me sobbing uncontrollably on the other end of the line.

Speaking with my aunt and family made Sheila's death more raw and painful. Sheila would never see her aunt again. She would never see her grandparents, any of her aunts and uncles, or her cousins. She would never see her father again. My heart ached horribly at the thought. I shook uncontrollably as I cried. I attempted to calm myself, to speak to my aunt, but I couldn't stop. It was a mourning I had not experienced before - the mourning of family.

In between my sobs, I heard my aunt crying quietly. It was shocking news to receive. But there was nothing I could do. There was no way to comfort my aunt or the rest of Sheila's family. I knew, painful as it was, that it was important to inform all the relatives and make sure the news got to Peter, if he was still alive. But telling the story ripped a hole in my chest.

I heard my aunt crying quietly. 'I'm so sorry to hear that,' she said, forcing out the words.

'So am I. I can't believe she's gone,' I said, as I wiped the tears covering my face.

'I will try and send someone with the message to your mum,' she said.

'Thank you, Auntie. Have a nice trip,' I said and hung up the phone. I told myself I didn't want to finish all of Muzhindu's phone credit. But in actuality, I didn't want to hear the mourning of my family any more.

The date of Sheila's burial was July 18. The news of what had happened had spread around the community. While some felt the same as the mob did about foreigners, many did not. The people who came to provide support amazed me. The Mayor, police chief, local pastors, and prominent business people all came to bury my little, innocent girl.

'It's so sad that we have all been brought together by such a tragic event' said the Mayor at the ceremony. 'In these difficult times when we black people are supposed to be united like brothers and sisters, it is so heartbreaking to see us wasting our energy fighting each other. South African people are known all over the world as welcoming, friendly, and loving. Then a select few among us decide to take the law into their own hands and ultimately tarnish the good image of this rainbow nation. This kind of behaviour should never be tolerated. It should never be allowed to happen again. Look at the pain it has caused in innocent families.

'I would like to take this opportunity on behalf of the nation to apologize and render our condolences to the Gapa family. I am glad that the chief of police is here. I would like to urge him to make sure that those responsible for such sickening acts are brought to justice. Thank you.' As he sat down, people clapped quietly.

It was then my turn. I was given an opportunity to say something, if I so wished.

'Before we were attacked, my daughter had told me that she was afraid she was never going to see her best friend and her father again. She was an intelligent, lovely little girl who didn't deserve to die like this. We ran away from political violence in Zimbabwe and thought we would find refuge here. This was a move I will regret the rest of my life. She was the most precious person to me.'

I put my hand over my heart, remembering the feeling of her little heart beating against my chest. Anger began to swell up inside me. 'It's been almost two months since my daughter was brutally murdered. Why is it that no one has been arrested, or even charged? I am reminded again that we as immigrants are not important. We are foreigners. *Amakwirikwiri*, as you call us. I beg you to not rest until those who did this to my daughter are put behind bars.' My voice had risen with malice and hate. In my head I could see the man who had killed my daughter. I wanted to say more, but felt it best to sit down.

Rachel's pastor came and offered some beautiful words. A few more people gave their thoughts, including the police chief, who promised to get the perpetrators of the crime. Finally, Sheila's coffin was lowered down into the ground as the choir from Rachel's church sang.

Gertrude was at my side, holding my hand as my little girl was put into the dark. The mayor approached me, offering his hand. I shook it. 'When you are available, come and see me. I would like to give you a letter that will help you apply for asylum.'

'Thank you,' I said. He nodded and walked back to his car. Everyone went back to their homes and we got into Muzhindu's car and headed back to his house. I had said my last goodbyes to my daughter. Peter was all I was thinking about now. I missed him so much and wished he had been next to me as they had laid our daughter to rest. His birthday had passed and I wondered how he had felt on his own on such a special day.

Besides Peter, there was something else on my mind. Something, aside from everything else I was coping with, that wouldn't allow me to sleep. After what Mugabe's militia had done to me, I was worried sick about what I could have contracted from them. I knew how easily STDs could spread and that it was possible to not show any symptoms while they destroy the reproductive organs. Every day and every night I thought about getting tested, but I was scared.

Early in the morning of Monday July 21, I thought about it carefully and made up my mind to get tested. I had to know. I took my handbag and went to the hospital on my own. I walked straight to the New Start Centre, the local lab that performed the test, where I was greeted by two very friendly female nurses. I explained to them what I wanted to be tested for. They made me feel relaxed and comfortable. I was glad they were female. If it had been a man, I would have found it very difficult to narrate what had happened in my life.

They asked me about my sexual and medical history. I had no choice but to tell them about the rape ordeal, as they wanted to know why I had decided to come for the test. They were upset and shocked by what Mugabe's militia had done to me. This was the first time I had opened up about the rape. It was hard and painful, as the events became fresh in my mind again, but was glad that I had talked about it with people who sympathized with me.

'The test we will do will determine whether you have any STDs, including HIV,' said one of the nurses.

'I understand,' I replied.

'We want you to know that you have made a very good decision,' said the other nurse. 'It's always best to think ahead, even in cases when there is only a slight chance of you ever having AIDS.'

The second nurse spoke. 'If you are HIV positive, you can take advantage of immune system monitoring, early treatment, good nutrition and hygiene. You can control the infection instead of letting it control you,' she said.

They went on and on about how I should not panic, that it didn't mean I was going to die the next day if I had the infection. They also repeated many times that there was help and support for me. *I know I won't die the next day. Just do the test.*

Finally, the waiting was over. They took some blood samples and started testing. I was glad they were going to tell me the results on the same day. I was told to wait outside as they wanted to see other people. After a while I was called back in.

One nurse looked at the other, and then back at me. 'The results show that you don't have any chlamydia, gonorrhea or herpes, but you tested positive for HIV.'

I stared at them, a blank look on my face. 'What?'

'You are HIV positive, Nyasha. We're very sorry, but we want you to take advantage of the benefits of knowing about this early.'

The room began to spin around me. I couldn't believe what I was hearing. I thought I would have something curable like herpes or chlamydia. HIV was not what I wanted to hear. I heard the nurses trying to talk to me. One eventually had me sit down while the other brought me a glass of water.

I took a small sip. 'I'm HIV positive? You're sure?' I asked, shocked.

One of the nurses nodded. 'There are many people that have lived with the disease for years, Nyasha. Because you've found out so early, you're at an advantage. You should be able to manage your health and the disease to live a full and happy life.'

I couldn't say anything. They continued with their instructions and comfort, but I didn't hear it. Peter had never been unfaithful, and I had tested negative before. When Peter had come back from his work in Harare, I demanded we get tested because I knew what men could do when they were away from their wives. We had also heard how prostitutes in these cities target lonely men. Peter didn't protest, as he wanted to prove that he had not been up to anything mischievous when he was away. Our trust even grew after we both tested negative. So I knew where I had got the disease.

The memories of that horrible night were fresh in my mind. The expressions of satisfaction, of triumphant conquest from each man flashed before my eyes. My anger and horror at what those men had done flooded through me. I jumped up, feeling claustrophobic, wanting to leave as soon as possible.

'Nyasha! Please calm down. Sit down. I know it is a lot to process, but we are here for you,' said one of the worried nurses.

'I need to leave. Thank you for giving me the news. I'll be sure to take care of myself, but I need to leave,' I said as I battled with the anger raging inside of me.

'We don't want you to concentrate on your past. We want you to look at the future and continue to live your life as normal as possible,' the other said.

I nodded, leaving the room. As I rushed down the hall towards the exit, I hurried away from every man I saw, thinking each one looked like one of the men who raped me. I was struggling to reach the hospital doors without falling over as I battled with horrible memories and tragic realisations of what that night had done to me. I was disgusted with those horrible men. Who could ever live with themselves after defiling someone in the most intimate way possible?

But I was also disgusted with myself. How could Peter ever want me again? How could I ever look at myself in the same way? I walked through the hospital doors and went home.

The next day I woke and took a shower. I didn't have any appointments, so I sat outside basking in the sun and thinking about what having HIV would mean. *Those animals didn't just destroy all I had, but they gave me HIV as well. How is Peter going to take this news? Will he ever want me back? Will he want to be with someone who could give him HIV?*

'Nice day isn't it?' said Rachel as she sat next to me.

'It is,' I replied.

'Are you OK?' she asked after noticing tears in my eyes.

'I'm fine,' I lied.

'Come on, Nyasha, you can tell me what it is.'

'Sure am fine.'

There was no way I was going to tell her about my new condition. We sat in silence. Our attention was taken by two little boys and two little girls who had come to play not far from where we sat. They frequently glanced at us, obviously scared of my monstrous face. They didn't know I was that once beautiful lady who had been their friend's mum.

One girl was missing from the group - Sheila. These were her friends. If she were alive, she would have been sitting among them telling the African tales I used narrate to her. I missed her so much. I remembered the day I had found her telling them about our experiences as we came to South Africa. *She must be missing her friends terribly. I wonder if she can see them. Can she see me? Can she see how torn apart I am without her?*

My thoughts were distracted by the arrival of Muzhindu, who was coming from the shops with a handful of groceries in his hands. Rachel jumped up and walked towards her husband, smiling. What a happy couple. Would Peter and I ever be like that again?

I remembered our happy days. I remembered our days before I gave birth to Sheila. Like a little girl I would jump up and run towards him every time he came home from cow herding. Spending those longs hours without him while he had gone with the cows was too much for me to bear. He was my best friend and the love of my life. I always wanted him by my side. We would sit together in our small hut and talk about our dreams for the future. It was romantic and special. I suddenly felt a longing for him I had never felt before. *I need him. If they can't get me any news about him I will have to go back and find him by myself.*

'Uncle! Is Sheila coming back today?' shouted one of the little girls.

Muzhindu didn't know how to answer her. She had

probably been told by her parents that Sheila had gone to visit someone somewhere. I understood, as most parents find it difficult to discuss death with their children. We all looked at each other, not knowing if we should lie to Sheila's friends.

One little boy walked over to her and whispered something in her ear. The little girl moved away, sat next to a peach tree and started crying. This was too much for me. I broke down and wept as well. Rachel went over and took the little girl into her arms. After I had calmed down, I told Rachel and Muzhindu that I felt it was a good idea for me to move out of their house. I couldn't stand looking at those little kids playing every day without Sheila by their side. It was like torture to me. They agreed, and I moved to Gertrude's place.

CHAPTER 20

On July 23 2008 I moved in with Gertrude and I continued to go back to the hospital for regular checkups and wound dressings. My wounds were healing very fast. I eventually decided to take advantage of the Mayor's offer. It was important to make my stay in this country legal, as it could open up many more opportunities for me and allow me to open a bank account.

Aside from what had just happened, I knew it was dangerous to keep money in the house. It also meant I would be able to look for a job rather than selling DVDs illegally, and Peter could join me. I had not given up looking for him, and as soon as my aunt came back from England she would give me the news about my husband. I felt so lonely and wanted him so desperately.

I went to see the Mayor and he gave me a very powerful letter, which I took to the Department of Home Affairs in Witbank. I filled out an asylum application and was given an appointment for October 1 for review.

By the time October 2008 came I had fully recovered, but I was now a totally different person. I didn't look like myself at all. My face was permanently deformed. It was covered in scars.

I woke up early in the morning and started preparing to

leave for my appointment. I waited for Gertrude to get ready, as she had said she wanted to accompany me. We took a taxi from her house to the long-distance taxi rank in Ermelo City Centre and jumped into a 15-seat taxi bound for Witbank. I was getting worried and impatient.

The taxi wouldn't leave with just the two of us. It had to be completely full, but no one was coming. We waited and waited. A few people started getting in.

'Just two more people and then we will be out of this place,' said Gertrude after seeing how uncomfortable I was becoming. She patted my knee.

'Why doesn't he just drive? We will definitely pick up two more people along the way,' I said. I looked at the driver, who clearly didn't care that some people in his taxi were in a hurry.

I didn't want to miss such an important appointment. It could change the course of my life. Every time I thought about the doors that could be opened if I were to become a legal immigrant, I became more and more anxious to get the taxi moving.

I couldn't stop checking the time on Gertrude's phone. There was still enough time to catch my appointment, but I had wanted to give myself a large window - you never knew what you would come across on the roads.

At last, to my relief, two tall, dark men jumped in and filled the two empty seats.

'Now, we'll be on our way,' said Gertrude, with a sigh of relief.

I too was relieved - until I looked at who the two men who had just got into the taxi. They were both looking at me oddly, seeming confused.

I jerked my head away and attempted to compose myself. I felt as if a hammer had smashed my chest. I couldn't breathe; anger started boiling inside me as I looked back at the first man who had got in. He was tall and very dark and was wearing a South African National team T-shirt and black jeans. He looked just like the man who had killed Sheila.

Although they had attacked us at night, the flames had lit up the area enough for me to see his face clearly. *It must be him,* I thought. *What kind of person is he? How could he be so cruel as to hit and kill an innocent girl who knew nothing about what they were demanding?*

I looked at him as he sat there giggling and joking with his friend. He sat there casually, as though the fact that he had killed a young girl didn't bother him at all. I was losing it. Rage was building up inside of me. If I had had a gun, I would have shot him right there.

I needed to get out of the taxi before I did something I would regret the rest of my life. I felt sick. I knew there was no way I was going to ride all the way to Witbank in the same taxi with the man who murdered my daughter.

'Excuse me, I need to get out. I'm sorry,' I said, as the driver was about to drive off.

'Nyasha! What are you saying? If we miss this taxi, we will never be able to get there on time,' said Gertrude, puzzled by what I wanted to do.

'What's wrong with you women? Are you serious? Do you know where you are going or what?' shouted the disappointed driver. I didn't reply. As soon as he had stopped the car, I hurried out and Gertrude followed.

'What is it, Nyasha?' asked the concerned Gertrude. 'I hope you understand the implications of what you have just done. You may not be able to get another appointment.'

Gertrude was upset, but she didn't know or understand and was waiting for an explanation. She didn't know what I was going through. My hands were shaking. I felt a lump rising in my throat. I couldn't talk. I couldn't breathe. I gasped for air, breathing hard. We watched as two other people jumped into the taxi, filling the seats we had vacated.

I took a deep breath. 'It's that tall, dark guy,' I said as I pointed at the leaving taxi.

'Which guy?' asked Gertrude as she looked around.

'The one who was sitting next to you,' I said.

'The one in the taxi? What's wrong with him?' she asked, looking confused.

'I think he is the one who killed Sheila,' I replied.

'What! Why didn't you say that before that taxi left? We have to go and tell the police,' said Gertrude.

'No, there's no point. It's a waste of time,' I said.

'Why would you say that, Nyasha?' she asked.

'I'm not completely sure. Besides, I don't think the police will do anything.'

'They will definitely do something. He killed a little girl. He can't get away with that!'

'How many months have gone by now since the death of my daughter? Not a single person had been charged for her murder. All the people who got arrested were released,' I replied.

'OK, let's get in the next taxi then. It's still important you get to the appointment,' said Gertrude.

'I have had enough of this. I want to go back home now,' I said as I started walking away.

Gertrude looked at me shocked as I began to walk away. I too was shocked by what I had said. She couldn't believe I was willing to throw away the opportunity either.

'Nyasha! Nyasha!' she shouted as she ran after me. I continued walking, becoming more resolved in my decision with each step. I knew I couldn't live in the country my daughter had been killed in. The memories were too painful and they were haunting me every day.

I felt Gertrude grab my arm. 'Nyasha, you need to think twice about this!'

'Gertrude, I *have* thought about it. I can't live in the same place my daughter was murdered. That memory haunts me every day. And now I see the man who killed my daughter walking freely in the streets! No, I can't live like this. I can't live in a place where people kill innocent children and get away with it.'

I hailed another taxi and we headed back to our house. Once we got through the door, I started packing my bags.

'So where do you want to go to now?' asked Gertrude.

'I told you, I'm going back home,' I replied.

'I thought you meant coming back here?'

'I meant what I said. It is too distressing to live here. It's best if I go back to Zimbabwe before I go crazy.'

'You are overreacting, Nyasha. Just relax, take some time to think this through. You don't want to make a decision you will regret forever.'

'The decision I regret was coming here in the first place. I hate this country. I hate the people of this country. I hate the system in this country. I don't care anymore about the opportunities this country is offering me. I just don't want to stay here. This is it. I am going home!'

'Life is still hard back home, Nyasha. Do you honestly think home will be any better? Think of what they did to us. You want to escape Sheila's murder. But we don't know what the men back home would have done if they had found Sheila, or Esther for that matter. They might have killed them as well, or worse. And those were men we knew. You'll run into them all the time, reminding you of what they did to you.'

'I know. But it is different for some reason. At least I have good memories back home, even if they are mixed with some horrible ones. I can't see how I can ever be happy here.'

'What are you going to do when you get there? How are you going to survive?' asked Gertrude.

'Well, I'm not sure. I can take the money I've already earned and at least go back to my home. Maybe Peter is there. Hopefully the house is still there. And at least the violence has stopped. They are talking about the changes that will be made to the government. I'm sure things will get better soon.'

'So you want to leave now?' she asked, eyeing the suitcase I was packing.

'I will leave first thing tomorrow morning,' I replied.

She could see that I had made up my mind and there was nothing she could do to stop me.

CHAPTER 21

Later, after I had finished packing, I went to thank Muzhindu and his wife for all the things they had done for me. They didn't receive the news of my plans with joy. They tried to persuade me to change my mind, but they couldn't do it. I had made up my mind, and there was nothing they could say that would make me stay.

My thoughts were now on Peter. I missed him so much. All I wanted was for him to wrap his arms around me, to tell me everything would be fine. But I knew that might never happen. I had failed to find out if he was still alive or not. My mother had said she would send someone to the village to see if he was still alive, but I never heard back. It was best for me to go and find out for myself.

From Muzhindu's place, I went to see the Mayor. He had worked very hard to get the money for Sheila's burial and it was appropriate that I should go and thank him as well. He had given me the remaining money he had raised for the burial, which I was now using to cover transport costs for my trip back home.

I got to his office and thanked him for everything. He was disappointed by my decision, but he understood that it was my life and I had to do what I felt was right.

From the Mayor's office, I went to thank Rachel's pastor. I told him to thank his congregation for me, since I wasn't going to wait for Sunday service. After that, I went back to Gertrude's place and rested.

Early in the morning on the next day, I got up feeling excited about the trip home. I couldn't wait to see Peter. I wondered how he would react to my new face. I started my preparations for the journey.

There was a knock at the door, and Gertrude went to see who it was. I was pleased to see Muzhindu and his wife walking in. They wanted to say one final goodbye, and offered to drive me to Ermelo City Centre.

Since I was riding in their car and wouldn't have to pay for a taxi, I decided to go and visit Sheila's grave one last time. I felt tears flow slowly down my cheeks as I said a silent goodbye to my precious little girl. *Goodbye, my darling. I'm sorry I couldn't protect you. I will love you always.*

From the grave, we went to the city centre. Saying goodbye to Gertrude, Muzhindu, and Rachel was hard, much harder than I thought it would be. They had become my family in South Africa. I don't know how I would have survived as long as I did without them. I embraced each of them individually, promising that I would stay in touch. I then took a taxi to Johannesburg. There was a fair amount of traffic on the roads, so it took about two hours to get there.

Most of the buses that were going to Harare were actually leaving in the evening, so I decided to book a seat on the Pioneer bus, which was leaving slightly earlier, at about five o' clock. I loaded my bags into the bus and then decided to see how the famous Johannesburg looked, since it would probably be my only chance to explore the city.

I went window shopping and bumped into many Zimbabweans who were buying things to resell back home. After a long walk, I was tired and decided to look for something to eat. There were so many restaurants in Johannesburg to choose from; I eventually picked one at random. I bought myself a plate of rice and beef stew.

As I was about to sit down, a dirty lady with torn clothes and shoes approached me.

'I am very sorry, my sister. I know I smell and I don't wish you to lose your appetite so I will go and wait outside. But please, if you happen to leave any food, remember me. I am hungry and would be more than happy to eat whatever you don't want,' said the dirty lady.

I raised my eyes to look at this lady who was begging so politely. My eyes widened. I couldn't believe who was standing before me. It was Happiness.

While I recognised her, she clearly did not recognise me. The deformity of my face had now become a reality to me, as my own dear friend could not recognise me.

'Don't go outside, come and join me. Sit down,' I said.

'But I smell so bad,' she said, glancing at the other customers.

'It doesn't matter, sit down,' I told her.

She looked shocked by my kindness. She sat down opposite me, but continued looking out the window. For what, I was not sure.

'Hey! Hey! Go outside! Don't disturb my customers!' shouted a man who was behind the counter.

'It's OK! She is not disturbing me,' I shouted back.

I took out twenty rands and gave it to her.

'Thank you,' she said.

'Go and buy whatever you want,' I said.

I looked at her as she staggered to the counter. She looked very hungry. I wondered when she had last had a proper meal. I tried to figure out what could have happened at the farm. Why was she here in such a state? And where was Titus? Did he survive? I was heartbroken by the way she looked. Whatever happened to them, they were clearly struggling.

I thought of Esther and Brighton. There was a big possibility that they were also here roaming the streets of Johannesburg, scavenging for food. I was desperate to ask her, but wasn't sure how. She came back with her own plate of rice and sat down.

'Why didn't you buy a drink?' I asked.

'I think it's wise that I keep this money. People like you are not easy to come by,' she replied.

I stood up and went to the counter. I bought her two Coca Cola cans and gave them to her. As I sat down, I couldn't decide if I should reveal myself or not. I desperately wanted to know how she came to be here, if Titus was alive, and if she knew anything about Brighton and Esther. But I didn't want to talk about Sheila's death, especially to someone who knew her. I didn't want to mourn Sheila all over again. If I revealed who I was, Happiness would surely inquire after Sheila's well-being and would mourn her loss. I wasn't willing to grieve for my daughter again. Not in a restaurant full of strangers. Peter was the only person I wanted to do that with. He was the only one who could understand my pain and give me comfort. My longing for Peter and my fear that he was dead was growing stronger every hour.

'Is this all for me?' she asked.

I nodded my head.

'Today is my lucky day. Thank you,' she said smiling.

'You are welcome,' I said.

'Hey,' she said, looking at me inquisitively. 'Your voice sounds very familiar.'

'Is that so?' I said.

'Yes. You sound like someone we came with when I was coming here,' said Happiness.

'So how did you end up here?' I asked, trying to distract her from what she was thinking.

'It's a long story, my sister. I ran away from a farm I used to work at and, since I didn't know anyone in this country, I found myself here with no one to help and nowhere to go to,' she said, eating her food quickly.

'So where do you sleep?' I asked.

'We sleep at the Central Methodist Church here in Johannesburg. There are so many homeless Zimbabweans who sleep there,' she replied. 'I hope you don't mind me asking what happened to you.'

'It's a long story as well, my sister. It would take me almost two days to explain it all,' I replied.

'I'm eating your food and asking you all these silly questions and I haven't even started by asking you your name. That's rude, please forgive me,' she said.

I paused, wondering what I should tell her. I looked around

and saw people staring at us. *If I reveal myself, her reaction would definitely attract more attention. Why can't these people mind their own business?* I was feeling uncomfortable with the eyes staring at us. I wanted to leave as soon as we finished eating and felt there wasn't enough time to tell her all that happened after we left the farm.

'I go by Many Faces,' I said as I remembered my discussion with Rachel about changing my name.

'What kind of a name is that?' she asked.

I thought about the name again and concluded that I did want to use it, at least for those I hadn't told my story to. I realised that with everything I had been through over the past months, I had changed. I had changed inside and outside. I wasn't that shy and reserved village woman any more. I had stood in front of hundreds of people and spoken about the life of my daughter on the day she had been laid to rest. 'I have gone through a lot in my life and it has resulted in me losing my looks – once I was beautiful. It has changed me from being shy and timid to outspoken and brave. Life is constantly throwing new experiences, challenges, and hardships in our path. And those events and struggles change who we are.

'As life changes the person I am on the inside, my face represents the person I am on the outside. Someone who is always learning and evolving from what life throws my way.'

Happiness gave me an odd look, not quite understanding what I was trying to say. I wasn't sure I understood it either. 'Anyway, my name is Happiness,' she said.

'Nice meeting you,' I said.

'Nice meeting you too, and thanks for all this,' she said.

'Are you alone? I've been meaning to ask you.'

'Oh, no. My husband is here. He is the one who helped me escape from the farm. He is searching for food as well. I'll bring part of this back to him with one of the Cokes. He'll be thrilled.'

I smiled, glad to hear Titus was all right as well. 'There is a friend of mine in Mpumalanga Province who I think will be able to help you,' I said.

'Are you sure? Would your friend really help us?' she skeptically inquired.

'Absolutely,' I responded.

'Are you not an angel sent from Heaven to help me?' she said as she touched me to feel my flesh.

'Many people have helped me in my life. God uses people to do His work,' I said.

'May God be with you in all you do,' she prayed.

'Amen,' I said. 'Write this phone number down and call her as soon as you leave this place. She is called Gertrude,' I said.

'Gertrude! Who exactly are you?' she mumbled as she stood up. 'Please excuse me; I need to go borrow a pen.'

She jumped up and ran to the counter to ask for a pen. She came back and wrote Gertrude's phone number down. I could see that she wanted to ask me more about my life, but time was running out quickly. I didn't have the time to narrate to her what had happened to Sheila and me.

'Call her today. Here is the money to make the call,' I said as I gave her another twenty rands.

'Thank you very much,' she said. 'But what should I say to her since she doesn't know me?'

'Tell her you are my friend, if you describe me to her she will know,' I said as I stood up to leave. 'I have to go now, take care of yourself.'

I was glad to see how happy she was now; she suited her name again.

As I left the restaurant I saw Titus and Happiness meeting up. She was speaking to him excitedly, and I saw a smile spread across his face. He looked slimmer than when I had last seen him. He was wearing a torn shirt, his trousers had holes on the knees and his shoes looked old and dirty. I could see that they really were struggling.

As my departure time drew closer, I started walking towards the bus rank to board my bus. Happiness and Titus, both in a cheerful mood, were sitting on the Ermelo taxi rank and knew she must have contacted Gertrude. They had obviously made some arrangements to meet.

I boarded my bus and, at 5 pm, it drove off. I was pleased to know that Happiness and Titus would now have a new and better life. I left Johannesburg feeling peace for the first time since my ordeal had begun.

CHAPTER 22

The bus journey went much faster than I thought it would, and by midnight we were at the Beitbridge border post. I was able to cross the South African side without any problems, as I just showed them the hospital letters and the letter the Mayor had written for me.

On the Zimbabwe side of the border, I was charged 100 rands for not having a passport. But at that moment, I was more than grateful for my job and the money the Mayor had raised for me. Without it, I wouldn't have been able to pay the fee and get home.

Later on, the customs officials came and told us to take all our bags out for inspection. I couldn't even count the number of bags and boxes that were in the bus because there were so many. To make a difficult task even more challenging, the bus conductors hadn't packed them well - they were simply thrown into the bus, making getting them out incredibly difficult. With only one conductor available to unload the bus, it was going to take much longer to unload.

All the passengers arrogantly walked out, saying it wasn't their job to help with the bags—they felt it was the responsibility of the single bus conductor to take all the bags and boxes out of the bus, since we had paid for the bus service.

Everyone ignored the bus conductor as he begged for help. I was too shy to be the only one to step forward and help.

'Wellington!' shouted the conductor, waving to someone behind us to help him. I assumed it was one of his mates.

'Excuse me,' said a male voice behind me.

The voice sounded familiar, so I turned around to look at the man. It was Wellington Maseko. The last time any of us had seen him was when he had left us in Beitbridge, afraid to swim across the Limpopo River. I smiled at him, expecting him to greet me excitedly.

'Can I please pass?' he said as he walked past me.

I realised then that he did not recognise me, obviously because of the scars on my face. I had almost forgotten that I now carried a new face.

Wellington reached the bus conductor and they got in and started taking our luggage out. I was surprised to see what he was doing, but was unsure why he was doing it. He had either failed to raise enough money to cross over to South Africa, or he had found this job enjoyable and decided to stay. I looked at him as he worked tirelessly, taking the passengers' heavy bags out for inspection.

After about forty-five minutes of hard work, they finished taking the bags out. The driver went to call the customs officer. The officer came and started inspecting our bags to make sure nothing was being imported into the country illegally and to make those who needed to pay a customs duty do so. All this time I was looking at Wellington, who was breathing hard, obviously tired from the hard work he had just done. I wondered if I should tell him who I was.

Once the customs inspection was finished, the mammoth task of putting the bags back into the bus was next. This time, people helped, since everyone was desperate to leave the border and get home.

'As you are all getting back into the bus, can you please kindly donate whatever you can to this young man who has helped us so much?' asked the bus conductor as we lined up to get back into the bus.

'I'm not giving him anything. The conductor is the one who is supposed to pay him,' said one lady who was in front of me.

I watched as many people got into the bus without giving him anything. Only a few people gave him something, but only a few coins at most. From what I could see, he didn't get more than twenty rands. I felt sorry for him as he stood beside the bus entrance, wiping the sweat from his brow after all the hard work he had done getting the luggage out of the bus. He looked very tired. I could see how frustrated he was at the rude people he had helped, who clearly did not appreciate the hard work he had just done for them.

I quickly jotted Gertrude's phone number down on a piece of paper and wrapped it with a twenty rand note. I could now see why he was still here. There was no way he was going to raise enough money to cross the border, especially with the kind of attitude the people he was helping had. He was obviously working from hand to mouth. I got to the bus entrance and gave him the twenty rands. He jumped with excitement and hugged me.

'Thank you! Thank you very much. No one has ever given me this much before. Thank you,' he said.

I didn't say anything. As he had been loading the bags I had debated whether or not to reveal myself to him. I had decided not to, for the same reason I did not reveal myself to Happiness. The hole in my heart created by Sheila's death would only be healed, at least in part, by Peter. Sheila's father needed to grieve for her. And I needed to grieve with my husband. It was the only way to move on. If I relived her death with anyone but him, the hole would only continue to grow.

I smiled and walked quickly inside the bus, fighting the tears that were about to overwhelm me. I sat down and watched as the tired but encouraged Wellington counted how much he had made from his labour. What a life, I thought. I was glad that at least he had not turned to anything criminal to raise money, as many young men in Beitbridge were doing.

He unrolled the twenty rand note I had given him and saw the note. I had written 'Call Gertrude Mabika now' followed by her phone number underneath.

I could see surprise written all over his face as he looked for me. I hid my face as he moved around the bus, looking for me through the windows. He couldn't find me and eventually gave up. He turned around and ran to a nearby phone box to make the call.

'Is everyone in? Is there anyone who hasn't gotten into the bus?' asked the bus conductor.

There was no response, which the conductor assumed meant everyone was in. He said something to the driver and the driver started the bus engine. I saw the excited Wellington coming out of the phone box with a huge grin on his face. He started running towards the bus but before he got near, the bus driver took off. I assumed he had talked to Gertrude and I knew Muzhindu would be happy to help him. Not only was he a kind person, but having another worker would boost his business. I was happy to know I had helped one of us hopefully come out of poverty to a better life.

We continued with our journey, driving through the night. I watched out of the window as the vast jungle raced pass the window. I couldn't help but think about my own journey in the jungle months before. I thought of Chiwoniso and the strength she had given me after going through such a terrible ordeal. I thought of her death, of the grief of Brighton and Esther. And I thought of crossing the river, with Titus almost not making it. I carried such terrible memories of what had happened in the jungle.

But there were a few good memories. I recalled Esther and Sheila, walking hand-in-hand through the forest, playing games together and listening to the fairytales and stories we all told them to make the time pass more quickly. The memories were difficult to recall, but I hoped one day they wouldn't give me so much pain.

Eventually I fell asleep, waking up as we arrived in Harare just after 6 am. I got off at the Road Port long-distance bus rank and walked to the corner of Samora Machel Avenue and Fourth Street, where rides were available that went to Murehwa or Mutoko. The thought of seeing my husband again excited me. Sadness and fear slowly crept in as I thought of the events I would be reminded of. I missed Peter so much. I couldn't wait to see him. I just prayed that he was still alive.

CHAPTER 23

I waited impatiently for transport to my village. If it hadn't been such a long way I would probably have walked. I couldn't wait to be in Peter's arms again.

After waiting for about thirty minutes, I jumped onto a pickup truck heading to Mutoko. I got off at the Nyamutumbu turn-off and started walking towards our village. I became more and more nervous as I approached the village. *Are the militia still there?* I thought. *Am I walking into more danger than when I left?*

While Gertrude had warned me that it could be more dangerous, I didn't allow myself to think about it until I had entered the village. I walked down the road hesitantly, on the watch for any odd behaviour or movement from the people I passed.

When I got to the Nyamutumbu village shops I found, sitting outside the shops under a tree, the old lady who had wanted our house burned down, Paidamoyo Zengeya. She was sitting with two other women I had never seen before, probably her relatives. In front of them were two jars of an African brew called Chibuku.

I decided simply to walk by, hoping to not attract any attention from them.

'Oh that's a shame, look at that lady,' said one of the women.

I felt their gaze on me but continued to walk, pretending I couldn't hear them.

'I don't have sympathy for people like that. Most people looking like that were burnt during the Chimurenga armed struggle after they had been identified as traitors, sellouts. You don't know how many deaths these kinds of people have caused,' said Paidamoyo.

I was infuriated. How could she make such a judgment on someone she didn't know anything about? It was such a sweeping assumption. I remembered the night the Mugabe militia came to our house and how she had called for our house to be burned down. With her cruel and mean heart, I wondered how many deaths she herself had caused. I was angry. I felt rage boil up inside of me. I wanted to grab her by her hair and bang her head on the tree they were sitting under.

'I think she heard what you said, Paidamoyo. She is looking at us,' said the other lady.

'So what? I'm not afraid of anyone in this village. If she dares to touch me, she will see what my boys will do to her,' said Paidamoyo arrogantly.

I stopped and looked at them. I was seething with anger.

'She has stopped and she is still looking,' said that other lady again, glancing away from me.

'Young lady, go. Your ugly face does not intimidate us. Go now before I lose my temper. Do we look like some kind of tourist attraction to you?' barked Paidamoyo.

'Paidamoyo Zengeya! Paidamoyo Zengeya! Take a minute

to listen to the things that come out of your mouth. At your age, you should be ashamed of yourself. What kind of example are you giving to the young ones?' I said. Then I walked off.

There was silence for a moment and then one of the women spoke up.

'She knows who you are, Paidamoyo!'

'Who are you?' shouted Paidamoyo. 'Come back here and say that to my face!'

I ignored her and continued walking. She would probably figure out who I was eventually if I stayed in the village, but I didn't care. For the moment, she was shocked, which was all I wanted. She was a cruel, cold-hearted, vicious woman. The fact that she was willing to put all of us, her neighbours and fellow villagers, into the hands of men who beat us, raped us and destroyed our families showed who she truly was. I was glad to have done something to shake her, even just for a moment.

I walked straight to the nearby shops. I was curious to see how the village had been doing since I had left. The shelves had been empty when we had come into town before. Food had been scarce and the villagers had worried about starving. I decided to check to see if food was more available. If so, I would buy Peter his favourite drink. Assuming he was still alive.

I walked into Chakanetsa Bar and Groceries, which sold food items at one end of the store and operated a small bar at the other. I went straight up to the bar counter, but I could feel the eyes of the men who sat in the bar staring at me. When I had felt men's eyes on me before, it had been because I was beautiful. But I was no longer amused, as my new face was drawing attention all the time because of its ugliness. Through my entire journey back home, I had seen people nudging each other, staring and, in some cases, whispering something about my new look. At times kids had run away, some even crying after looking at my face. I was sure they thought I was some kind of monster coming to eat them up.

I waited at the bar for service, as there were already two people in front of me waiting to be served. A song by one of Zimbabwe's best dance hall artists started playing and two young men jumped on to the dance floor. They sang loudly along to the music and danced, causing everyone to watch them. I was shocked and infuriated. They were Adamson and Fadzi, two of the group of men who had raped me. These same boys had kicked and dragged Peter back to the school. And now here they were enjoying life to the full, eating, drinking and dancing.

Usatombo denha hako Mafia rangu
Tinokurova ukaita chitunha
Mbama yacho inorwadza kunge yeGudo
Ikakubata Iwe unotosura
Saka iwewe usafambe uchizvibhiga
Sasi rako rese ndirikurinzwa
Uchitaura kuti unondihwinha
Zvezvi bhakera ndini nhamba hwani
Kunyangwe zvako uri zimhitsa
Matunduru ndino kugara
Usanditarise uchindishora
Mambo wemughetto ndini
Kana ndichitaura mese nyararai

CHAPTER TWENTY THREE

Ndikatsamwa mese mapera
Handiregerere ende tsitsi handina
Chigaro changu hapana anonditorera
Zita rangu munori ziva mese

Don't cross us Mafias
We will beat you until you die
Our slap is as painful as that of a baboon
If it catches you, you will fart
Don't walk around saying you are big
I've heard all your rumblings
Saying that you will beat me
As far as fighting is concerned, I am number one
Even though you are muscular
I will sit on your chest
Don't you ever look down on me
I am the king of the ghetto
When I speak you all must listen
If I get angry, you are all finished
I don't forgive and I don't sympathize
My kingdom no one can take away
You all know who I am

They sang along at the tops of their voices, clearly not caring about the other customers.

'I think you have an admirer, Fadzi!' said Adamson as he pointed his finger towards me.

'Shut up! Who would want such an ugly woman?' said Fadzi.

I was so overwhelmed with anger and fear that I didn't even see that it was now my turn to be served. These were two of the men who were responsible for all the pain my family and I were going through. While I had lost my daughter, my best friend, my beautiful face and possibly my husband, they were here having a great time singing and dancing, not caring that both my family and others' families were full of suffering and pain because of what they had done.

The memories of that horrible, sad night played back in my mind over and over. As I saw them swinging their hips back and forth to the music, I couldn't help but remember their hips going back and forth on top of me, violating me in the cruellest way possible. I began shaking, unable to move or stop staring at them.

'Madam, are you all right?' called the lady who was behind the counter. Her question snapped me out of my thoughts.

'Sorry, I didn't hear you calling,' I said.

'Do you want to be served or what?' asked the lady, looking frustrated. She must have been calling me for a while.

'How much is it for a bottle of Coca Cola?' I asked.

'I don't have any change, so if you have a coin, it is five rands or, if you have US dollars, it's fifty cents.'

'I want two, but I don't have empty bottles and I want to take it away. I will bring back the empty bottles later,' I said.

'You will have to pay a deposit, which is a dollar per bottle,' said the lady.

'I want to pay with rands, so how much will the total come to?' I asked.

'That will be thirty rands in total,' she replied.

I reached for my handbag to get the money out. As I was about to open it, the horror of that night hit me again. This time I could see Fadzi on top of me forcing himself in as four guys pulled my legs apart and held my hands down. I felt sick. The pain of that memory was beyond description. I couldn't breathe. I felt as if I was about to have a heart attack. I grabbed my chest, trying to force my own breath in and out of my lungs. I felt dizzy, knowing I would likely fall to the floor. I ran out of the shop for fresh air.

'Ah! Where are you going now? Have I said something wrong?' shouted the cashier, but I ignored her.

Outside, I took a deep breath and tried to calm myself down. But I couldn't. I felt I was going crazy, that I was back in that school so many months ago. I realised that I had left my bags inside the shop. I hesitated. I didn't want to look at those boys again.

I shook my head, willing the memories to leave. I gathered some strength, turned around, and briskly walked towards my bags. Some of the other customers burst into laughter. Apparently, me running out and coming back in was funny to them. But they didn't know who I was. To them, I was some crazy, deformed woman who could hardly speak. They didn't recognise me because of the burns on my face. They didn't care why I was acting the way I was. They figured, I was sure, that I was simply mad.

I grabbed my bags and ran back outside, making everyone burst into laughter again. I stopped outside the door and rested my head on a post.

'So who is she afraid of here?' asked Adamson laughing.

'*Kupenga hakuridzirwe pito* [Madness does not need a referee to blow a starting whistle for you to start. It just starts]!' said Fadzi giggling.

'She is scared of the cashier's face,' retorted Adamson.

'I told you many times that this cashier is the ugliest woman in this village,' said Fadzi, laughing as they both approached the cashier.

'*Mazvimbirwa nedoro manje* [You have had too much to drink]. Leave me alone!' shouted the cashier.

'And if we don't? What are you going to do, bitch?' I heard Adamson cursing. I looked through the window and saw him moving towards her.

'Hey Adamson, leave her alone,' said another man as he pulled him back.

'She says I have had too much to drink. Did she buy me any beer?' asked Adamson, upset.

'Don't worry, just cool down my friend,' said the man.

'She needs to watch how she talks to me. I am not one of her good-for-nothing boyfriends,' said Adamson.

'It's OK, it's OK, she has heard you,' said the man.

'She can bring all her boyfriends and brothers. We will beat them up!' shouted Fadzi.

'Don't play with Ninjas!' shouted Adamson.

The cashier's face was pale. She was clearly frightened. Adamson and Fadzi were so puffed up and arrogant. I had heard enough. I couldn't be near them any more. I was frightened. I was seething with anger. The pain I felt was unbearable. I took my bags and began walking. It was time I went home.

CHAPTER 24

I had gone only a short distance from the shops when I saw a small girl walking towards me. The bounce in her step looked familiar. I looked at her face and couldn't believe what I was seeing. I thought I had to be dreaming. Surely it was Esther, Sheila's best friend, the adopted daughter I had abandoned at the farm?

A warm feeling filled my heart. Seeing her turned the sorrow and hurt which had clung to me after my encounter with Adamson and Fadzi into joy.

She slowly walked towards me and the closer she came, the more her looks came into focus. I wasn't dreaming. It really was Esther. I was shocked to see her in the village, but so glad to find her well and alive.

I dropped my bags, and she looked up at the sound. Scared by my new face, she tried to take a different road.

'Esther! Esther! Esther!' I shouted with excitement.

She stopped and turned towards me, looking a little scared.

'Who are you?' she asked timidly.

I remembered that I was now changed. She too had not recognised me. I couldn't tell her who I was, not yet, because she would want to know where Sheila was.

'How is your father?' I asked.

'Do you know my father?'

'Yes I know your father. He is called Brighton Mamombe and I know who you are as well,' I replied.

'How come I don't know you? Are you one of our relatives? Did you know my mother?' she asked.

'Yes I know your mother very well too,' I replied.

'Do you know that she is dead?' she said.

'I'm sorry to hear that. Was she sick?' I asked, pretending I didn't know what had happened.

'My father said I should not tell anyone what happened to her,' she replied.

'Good girl. You must always do what your father tells you,' I said.

'But your voice sounds very familiar' she said.

'Really? Who do I sound like?' I asked.

'My best friend's mum' she replied.

'What is your best friend's name?' I asked, surprised that she remembered my voice.

'Sheila. I miss her so much,' said Esther.

'Oh really? So where is this friend of yours now?' I asked.

'My father said I should not tell anyone about that either,' she replied. 'I have to go now, otherwise my uncle will not be happy if I bring the bread late to him.'

'Bye,' I said as I watched her run past me towards the shops.

I imagined Sheila running beside her. I was heartbroken. I sat on my bags and started crying. I thought of what she had said about Sheila. I could hear her words echoing in my mind again and again. I wondered how she was going to take the news of the death of her best friend.

As I sat there, I saw a woman coming towards me and I got up. I didn't want to cause a scene with my crying. I wiped my tears, grabbed my bags, and started walking towards my house.

After going only a short distance, I could see my home. In many ways, it was good to be back. This was where I was from. It is what I knew. But in so many ways, being home brought great sadness. As I looked around, I could see my home, but it wasn't the same. Our bedroom had been burned down and part of the roof and door were missing. The kitchen must have been burned as well, as the roof thatching was new. Someone had repaired it; I wondered who. Either Peter had repaired it or perhaps it had been taken over by Zanu PF's militia.

While I was thinking all this, I saw something crawling out of the kitchen. I at first assumed it was an animal, but as it continued moving, it looked human. As I looked more closely, I could see it was a grown man. I was too far away to clearly see the man's face. I stayed back, observing him, trying to figure out who he was. I was hesitant, unsure of what to say or do. If this were Peter, I wouldn't know how to speak to him. I had been so concerned about what he would think when he saw my altered face. But he had suffered as well. Perhaps he wasn't able to walk because of what those men had done. What would I say to this new Peter - the Peter who had stayed and suffered so much so Sheila and I could escape?

He crawled into the burned bedroom and I walked closer, attempting to get a better view. After a while he came out holding something. He paused, seeing that there was someone approaching. He sat down and looked at me. When I saw his face, peace and joy filled my heart. The feelings of doubt melted away. Peter - my husband! He was still alive. So this is what they did to him.

Explanations could come later. The fact that I had found him alive was all that mattered. I smiled, but he didn't smile back. He couldn't recognise that behind the burned mask was Nyasha, his once beautiful wife.

'Can I help you?' asked my husband.

Just hearing the sound of Peter's voice again made me cry with joy. I burst into tears, covering my face. He looked at me strangely, obviously shocked I was crying.

'Is everything OK?' he asked.

I wiped my tears. 'Peter!' I sobbed.

He looked at me with his mouth wide open.

'Nyasha! Nyasha! Is that you, my wife?' he screamed with excitement.

I nodded my head. The fact that he had recognised my voice made me cry more. I ran towards him as he crawled towards me as fast as he could, crying as much as I was. I got to him and knelt down, and we embraced. Wrapped in each other's arms, we cried for some time.

'I missed you so much Peter!' I said, still sobbing.

'I missed you too,' he replied, stroking my hair.

He pulled me back, holding me at arm's length, looking at me.

'What happened to you? What did they do to you? Your mother said you were dead!' .

I told him the story of what the mob had done to me.

'I should have died. I never thought I was going to see you again. But God has spared me,' I said.

CHAPTER TWENTY FOUR

'Where is Sheila?' he asked.

I looked down, not knowing how to tell him. I was silent. Peter understood, looking at me with a crestfallen face.

'I'm sorry Peter, she didn't make it,' I replied at last.

He crawled a little bit away from me, sat down and covered his face. And then, my husband began to wail. His grief, his sadness, flooded forth with every cry he made. I sat down next to him, wrapped my arms around his shoulders and joined in his tears. We sat like this for some time, mourning the loss of our daughter together.

'So you can't walk now?' I asked eventually, when our tears had at last run out.

'They damaged my spine. I couldn't walk and I wasn't moving when they finished beating me, so they left me for dead. They came back here, took everything, and then they burned our house down. Luckily, I was picked up by the headmaster of Nyamutumbu Primary School the following morning and he rushed me to Musami Hospital.'

He paused for a while. I could see that recalling the events of what they did to him was painful.

'I saw Adamson and Fadzi at the shops when I was coming here,' I said, looking down.

Peter stroked one of his hands across my scarred cheek.

'I'm sure it must have been awful, seeing those men after what they did to you,' said Peter.

'If I had had a gun, I would have shot them. I will never let them get away with what they have done to us,' I said, upset.

Peter was silent for a moment, clearly deep in thought. I didn't interrupt.

'I see them every day,' he said, eventually. 'They pass

through this place when they are coming home from the shops in town. I used to feel pain, hatred and fury every time I saw them. What they did was horrible, evil. But after a while, when it was clear they weren't going to try anything again, I realised that I was doing more harm to myself wallowing in my anger while they were clearly enjoying their lives. I had to move on and not let what happened define the type of person I am. I have put everything in God's hands, as those men clearly think they are above this earthly law. I won't have vengeance in my lifetime, but God will have His.'

I stared at him, shocked. My husband amazed me with his bravery and strength, with his ability to move past what happened. With the anger I felt, I knew it took an amazing amount of courage for him to be able to move on with his life without hatred or the desire to get revenge. *Should I do the same? Should I forgive them?* I wondered. The thought made me cringe.

The scars they had left would be with us for the rest of our lives. Rubbing shoulders daily with the perpetrators of such horrific acts would be like rubbing salt on ours wounds again and again. Forgiveness wasn't going to be easy, of that I was sure.

I wondered where Peter had got the strength to live under such conditions. Coming face to face with my daughter's killer had made me leave South Africa. I couldn't see myself being able to forgive them. Time can perform wonders, though. Perhaps, in time, I would learn to put everything behind me as well.

'Brighton told me about your journey to South Africa,' said Peter.

'It was hard, painful, and tragic. I actually saw Esther when

I was coming here. I had left them at the farm. Did he tell you how they ended up coming back?' I asked.

'Brighton has had a rather tragic story since returning home. He said that he worked very hard at the farm and managed to save some money. When he thought he had enough to move on and start a new life, he told the farm owner he wanted to leave, which was a mistake. He took Esther, Edwin, Ruramai, Tafara and Zvanyadza with him. They all left the farm early one morning. The farm owner, knowing their intentions, called the police and they were arrested just after leaving the farm. They attempted to run, but didn't make it. In the chaos of the police coming after them, there was gunfire. One of the policemen was shot. They were detained and deported the next day. With the little money they had saved, they took a bus from Beitbridge back here,' said Peter.

'That farm owner was very cruel,' I said.

'There's more. When Brighton and Esther returned, they weren't home long before the police came and arrested Brighton.'

I gasped. 'For what? What could he have done?'

'The farmer apparently told the police in South Africa that Brighton had been the one to shoot the policeman. They told the police here, who decided to arrest him.'

'Brighton would never do that!'

'He didn't. None of the men in that group had a gun. Someone else shot the officer. The farmer wanted revenge on Brighton for taking so many of his workers away from the farm.'

'Where is he now? Who is taking care of Esther?'

'Brighton is being held at the police station in town. Some

of the neighbours have been helping with Esther. We can go down to see him later, if you'd like.'

With Brighton in prison, I knew I needed to see him. I needed to make sure Esther was taken care of.

'Yes, let's do it.'

We went into the kitchen, where I told him about the rest of the journey from the farm to Ermelo, including everything else that had happened and about all the people who had helped us. He told me about how he had coped and about all the help he had received from our church members. They had raised his hospital fees and brought him food every day, since he couldn't do things on his own.

I was feeling rather torn as we brought each other up to date on our lives since being apart. I wanted to see Brighton and my mum, but I also wanted to be with my husband. Having been apart for so long, we deserved some time with each other. I was relieved that he was genuinely glad to have me back, although I had been raped and burned and was now the ugliest woman in Nyamutumbu instead of the most beautiful. I knew Peter was a good man and would have acted happy either way. But I could see the love for me in his eyes as we spoke. He looked at me as he had done the day we were married. For him, nothing had changed.

Evening came; we ate and went to bed. Being next to the man I loved felt like the most natural thing in my life. I was glad God had spared his life. If I had found him dead, I wasn't sure what I would have done. I probably would have taken my own life. Without him and Sheila, what else would there have been to live for?

CHAPTER 25

When I awoke the next day I decided to visit my mum first. I didn't know whether my aunt had sent a message to her or not. It was important that I put the old woman's mind at rest, since she thought I was dead. Peter couldn't move easily, so I had no choice but to leave him behind.

I walked to the main road and took a taxi that was heading to Marondera. After about fifteen minutes of driving I got off at the Kasino turnoff. From there to my parents' place was about eight kilometres, so I decided to wait for another taxi. I waited for an hour, but there were no cars going towards our village. Eventually I decided to walk, as I was eager to see my parents. It was very hot for such a long walk but I didn't mind. Over the last couple of months, I had walked much greater distances.

At last my parents' huts came into view in the distance. The thought of seeing my mum again filled my heart with joy. At that moment, I had almost forgotten about my new face. I remembered the last time I had heard her fragile voice, sobbing and praying to God to save me. I had told her how much I loved her and that it was the last time she would hear my voice. It must have been a horrible thing for her to go through, especially at 65. I wondered how she would react when we saw each other again. My parents had been blessed with five kids

- four boys and a girl. As I was the only girl, my mother loved me to bits.

It felt good to be back in the place where I had grown up. The paths, the trees, even the rocks on the side of the road all brought back memories. Many of those memories were with my friend Chiwoniso. A memory of us running in and out of the trees, trying to catch each other, flashed through my mind. I couldn't believe that she really was gone. I planned on offering my condolences to her parents before I left for home.

My parents' huts were located in such a way that there was no way you could avoid passing by the Kasino village shops if you wanted to get to their home. As I walked past them, I noticed plenty of eyes staring at me. I knew most of them, since I had grown up here, but they couldn't recognize me with my deformed face.

In front of the bar, in the middle of the shops, were four elderly men, including my father, sitting with a jar of African beer in front of them. My father was wearing his favourite sisal hat, brown trousers and a nicely-ironed blue shirt. My mother always made sure her husband looked good. He looked at me but failed to recognise his once beautiful daughter behind the charred mask of my face.

I walked past the men and after a short distance the compound was in sight. I saw my mum sitting outside, basking in the sun with Tendai, my 10-year-old nephew, next to her. They looked at me with curiosity and apprehension as they tried to recognise who I was. They stared at me with worry written on their faces, obviously wondering why I was intruding without saying anything.

'*Makadiiko?* [How are you?]. *Tinga kubatsirei nei?* [Can we help you?]' enquired my mother.

I didn't reply. I burst into tears. I remembered when that fragile voice had pleaded with God to have my life spared. With the love she had for me I wondered how she had coped, thinking that I was no more. I ran towards her and embraced her, still crying.

'Amai vaSheila! Amai vaSheila! Is it you Amai vaSheila? Is it really you Amai vaSheila?' screamed my mum with excitement.

'Yes, Mum, it's me,' I sobbed, amazed that she had recognized me so quickly.

'God you are so good! Oh God, I thank you!' she sobbed.

She knelt down and started praying. She was so overcome with emotion. She was elated. My joy was short-lived, however, as I thought of the bad news I would have to give her.

'Tendai, run, go and call your grandpa,' she said as she sat down next to me.

She looked at me and touched my face.

'Is this what those criminals did to you?'

'Yes, but the most important thing is that I am alive.'

She felt the scars in my face and hands. I looked at her as tears started flowing down her cheeks.

'Does it still hurt?'

'No, the wounds are completely healed now,' I replied.

'Where is Sheila? Why didn't you bring her with you?'

I looked at her; tears had also started streaming down my cheeks. I opened my lips but the words couldn't come out.

'No! No! No! Tell me it's not true!' she said, crying.

'I'm so sorry, Mum! They killed her, they killed my little innocent girl,' I wept.

My mum screamed in agony. I joined her as we mourned my daughter. The sobbing was so loud that it reached our neighbours. Within a short while people started coming over, curious to find out what was wrong. They all sat down with us for a while, offering their support when they learned what had happened to my precious daughter.

I noticed the neighbours beginning to move aside to allow someone to approach us; my father, clearly saddened by hearing the news. He knelt down next to me. I wasn't sure what he was doing; my father and I had never been close. But he took my hand and held it in his. I looked at his face and saw tears forming in his eyes. He looked up and we stared at each other. No words needed to be spoken. My father was grieving for me and my daughter. In his own way, he was providing me comfort. I squeezed his hand as my parents and I bid farewell to a special daughter and granddaughter.

Later in the afternoon I felt it was time I went back. I went to Chiwoniso's parents to offer my condolences. I sat with them for a while before heading for the main road to look for a taxi to take me back to my husband.

When I arrived I saw Peter in tears, holding one of our family portraits. I knew that mourning our loss was going to take a long time. I cried as I looked at the photo of Sheila smiling, sitting on a chair while Peter and I knelt beside her. I wished the beauty I had once had could have been restored, but more than that I wished for my daughter. Life without Sheila was proving to be difficult for us.

Later that evening, after I had calmed down, I prepared dinner and ate with my husband. We were missing Sheila. Our home was quiet and sad without her. We were used to her praying before we ate each meal and we felt her absence deeply as we ate dinner. Peter was trying to put on a brave face, but I could see he was in pain and was struggling to accept that our little angel was no more.

After a silent dinner, we decided to go to bed. We just lay there next to each other in silence. I wondered what was going through Peter's mind. He turned to face me and looked at me for a while. He put his hands on my face, tracing the scars with his fingers. His eyes shone with love as I watched him feel my hideous face. Slowly and gently, his hands started going down. He got to my breasts and squeezed them. I jumped, shocked by what he was trying to do. I became irritated rather than aroused. I wanted him to stop, but I didn't want to upset him. He slowly moved down to my groin, then to my hips. I closed my eyes as the thoughts of the last time a man had touched me came to my mind. I felt angry and ashamed. I thought of another important issue I had not discussed with Peter. I grabbed his hands and looked at him.

'I'm sorry, I can't,' I said.

'It's OK, I understand,' he said.

I got up and sat down at the edge of the bed.

'What's wrong?' he said, as he struggled to get up. He got up and put his arm around me.

'There is something I have to tell you,' I said, as I covered my face with my hands. This was painful, but he needed to know.

CHAPTER TWENTY FIVE

'It's OK,' he assured me.

'I had a test done before I came back to you. I am HIV positive.'

He was quiet for a while. He covered his face with his hands, shaking his head. He looked upset and shaken by the news. We knew where the infection had come from. After he had calmed down, he thanked me for having the courage to tell him. I told him about all the counselling I had received and what precautions we were to take. He promised to stand by me and support me. I was glad to have such a man by my side.

He hugged me as I sobbed, lamenting that I had been ruined, scarred both inside and out by such a horrible ordeal. He spoke comforting words in my ear, reminding me how much he loved me, no matter what happened.

We rested, wrapped in each other's arms for some time, eventually falling asleep.

The next day in the morning we were visited by Tafara Kaseke, his wife Zvanyadza and their son Evans, who was on a two-week break from his music tour. He had bought a small car which he wanted to show his parents. I was thrilled to see them. They explained to me all that had taken place at the farm after we had escaped. We told them of our plans to visit Brighton and their son offered to take us to where he was locked up.

When the afternoon came, we journeyed into town to see Brighton. Peter had to drag himself from the car park into the police station. I felt sick, seeing my husband reduced to such difficult, pathetic circumstances. It took him some time to get from the car park into the police station, but I wore a proud face the entire time. My husband was an amazing man to have got through what he did. I was proud to stand next to him. Many of our neighbours looked at him with pride and sympathy as well. He was a survivor, and so was I.

We entered the police station and were taken to Brighton. Esther was visiting him as well. He greeted everyone enthusiastically, but he didn't recognise me at first. Once he realised who I was, I could see how difficult it was for him to look at my new face.

It was hard to break the sad news to Esther, especially since she still struggled to recognise me. She broke down and cried when she realised who I was. After I had comforted her, I asked her to go and play with a doll she had brought, at the front of the station near the police officer. She reluctantly agreed to leave.

It was time to discuss another issue that I was more passionate about now, after knowing Brighton's current predicament, than ever. Peter and I had discussed it at the house as we had lamented over his broken spine and my HIV diagnosis. Brighton, however, beat us to it.

'My friends, I believe I know what you are going to ask. Nyasha had asked me before when she left that horrible farm. She told me about the promise she had made to my wife before she died. Nyasha promised to take care of Esther as if she was her own daughter.'

He looked at me intensely. 'When we were at the farm, Nyasha, I was able to take care of my daughter. Regardless of the horrible conditions, I was able to keep her safe. But now, I have no idea how long I'll be here. And I need someone to take care of Esther. I need good people to be parents to her when I cannot be.'

I couldn't wipe the smile off of my face.

'Of course, Brighton.'

'She will be our daughter, Brighton, as she will always be yours,' Peter replied.

Brighton smiled. He was glad of the news, but I could see the sadness in his eyes at the thought of giving his daughter to someone else.

'Esther, come back, please,' Brighton called.

Esther skipped over, her doll in hand.

'Yes, Papa?'

'Esther, would you like to go and stay with Auntie Nyasha and Uncle Peter?' asked Brighton.

'Oh yes! That will be nice. I would love that,' replied Esther, making me smile even more. 'How long will I stay there?'

Brighton put on a brave face, attempting to cover his grief with a smile.

'My darling, I'm not sure how long I'll be here. Nyasha and Peter love you as much as I do. They will take care of you and keep you safe.'

Esther's face fell. 'But, Papa, will I still be able to see you?'

I put my arm around Esther. 'Of course you will. You can see him every day, if you'd like. We'll never replace your real parents, Esther. But we'd like to be your second set of parents, if you'd let us.'

Esther didn't make any reply. She merely wrapped her arm around me, giving me a small but strong hug. I knew that was a yes.

'I realised the day you left the farm how close you two had become and what you meant to her' said Brighton. 'She never stopped crying for you. I know you will look after her well, like your own daughter. I know the promise you made to my wife that night. I know you'll take this opportunity to fulfill it.'

'Thank you so much' I said, giving Esther a hug.

Using the money I had brought from South Africa, we began rebuilding our lives. We repaired our bedroom. We were able to hire some young men in the village to do the repairs. Our friends and church members chipped in, donating whatever they could with cash, food items and their time. Some of our friends organized a rotation among friends and church members for one person to help me in the field each day, as Peter was not able to do much. I was truly grateful for their help. Because of the assistance we received, we were able to keep food on the table and bring some money home with the produce we were able to sell. We would not have been able to survive without them.

After a week, we had finished repairing our bedroom and Esther moved in. The memory of Sheila was always with us. I heard her voice as I was preparing dinner. I saw her bounding over to Peter each time he came into the kitchen. Sheila's death was a hole in my heart that could never be filled. But having Esther with us was our saving grace. She was a patch placed over that hole in my heart, lessening the pain of losing our daughter. She brought a joy, a lightness of spirit, that made our lives, so full of sorrow and tragedy, find happiness and hope in the future.

EPILOGUE

I have written this book not because of my opposition to Zanu PF or as a way to push my campaign for MDC, but because of my strong opposition to political violence, to the rape of women, men and children, and to abuse of any kind, especially against women and children. I hope, by showing the pain that I and my family have gone through because of political violence, it will help our leaders of tomorrow move away and shun any group that condones such actions.

There are many things our government needs to do to protect vulnerable woman and children. Many abused women and children would find their lives in danger if they came out into the open to report abuse. For example, Nyembesi Gavhure, an 18-year-old girl of Mutenda village in Masvingo, was killed in December 2008. On April 27 2011, the Zimbabwean Herald published a story with a headline, 'Unrepentant Rapist Allegedly Kills Victim.'

The article stated that 28-year-old Victor Mukwaturi of the same village had been arrested for raping Nyembesi Gavhure and detained at Muchakata Police Station. However, he had escaped and gone to look for Nyembesi. He had found her and marched her to a nearby mountain, where he had allegedly killed her before fleeing to South Africa. Thanks to this and many other similar stories, the number of silent victims of rape is on the rise.

It is appalling to learn that xenophobic attacks are still being carried out today. On June 12 2011, the Zim diaspora newspaper carried a headline that read, 'HORRIFIC VIDEO OF SOUTH AFRICANS KILLING A ZIMBABWEAN'. It alleged that for the first time, the South African media had published a video entitled 'A Burning Hatred' of a racist attack on a 26-year-old man who had been brutally murdered in Diepsloot on YouTube.

Farai Kujirichita's crime was that he was a Zimbabwean. Surrounded by a jeering mob, he was bludgeoned to death. His horrifying final moments were captured on a video which thrust South Africa's violence back into the international spotlight. Farai was being pushed and pulled. His captors ordered him to throw himself into the flames of the burning shop. He broke free, tried to run away, but fell down and the mob was on him. Farai was still alive when a man in a white cap methodically destroyed his face and skull with a heavy wooden plank. He was probably (or hopefully) dead or dying by the time another man grasped his belt and punched him repeatedly in the groin. A grinning teenage girl raised a large chunk of cement above her head to finish him off. After some time, the police finally arrived. They kept the mob from setting Farai on fire and were there as he drew his final breath.

I cried when I saw this video on You Tube. I watched in horror as they hit the innocent Farai again and again. They killed him as they would kill a snake. It brought all those memories of my daughter's death back again.

On May 12 2011 I was pleased to read in the *Zimbabwean Herald* that the Zimbabwean cabinet had approved the Zimbabwean Human Rights Commission Bill. The bill seeks to make provision for the powers and operation of the Zimbabwean Human Rights Commission. If adopted, the Zimbabwean Rights Commission Act would empower the commission to investigate people in their individual capacities, state and corporate institutions.

My happiness soon turned to sadness when I heard our minister's announcement that the commission would carry out investigations only into alleged acts of violence which had occurred after February 2009. That ruled out my case and the cases of all those who were attacked in 2008. This means we will have to continue rubbing shoulders and coming face to face with our attackers on a daily basis.

More than four years has passed since our ordeal, yet I am still haunted. I want to forgive and forget, as Peter has done, but it is hard when you see your attackers daily, acting as though they had never done anything wrong. I believe the only way I will be able to move on with my life is when these barbarians are locked behind bars where they belong.

The government is planning to hold elections again this year to decide who should rule the country. I fret at the thought of what these thugs might do to us and other innocent young women in our village as the elections start up.

Life has been difficult since coming home. After some time, my health deteriorated and I went in for a checkup. They tested my blood and found that my CD4 count, which measures the strength of my immune system, had gone down. As HIV can destroy CD4 cells, this was a concern. They have now put me on anti-retroviral tablets and things have improved.

Aside from the trials, there are many positive things that have happened in my life. Peter has been having physiotherapy, and we believe one day he will walk again. We had been worried about expenses in the beginning, as Peter could no longer work with his injuries. We switched places for a short time, with Peter staying in the home with Esther and me working in the fields. This was difficult for both of us. But, amazingly, our friends stepped in. Edwin and Tafara take turns assisting me in the fields each day. Zvanyadza and Ruramai help with the household duties and Esther, allowing me to assist in the fields as much as possible. Esther is now going to school and is top of her class. She is the most brilliant student in her age group.

Her father, Brighton, was released from jail after an official from the city came to our village, heard his case and determined that it was unlawful to detain him. When Brighton was released, he had a long talk with Esther. She had been happy with us while Brighton was in jail, so she asked if she could stay with us and Brighton agreed. Esther sees him every day and our hearts are full of the love we feel towards this little girl.

Brighton has found true love again and is now happily married. They are expecting their first baby in three months' time. Peter and I are waiting for our passports, which we applied for last week. If they come, we will be travelling to South Africa to show Peter and Esther where I buried Sheila. Gertrude and our loving friends in South Africa are paying the expenses for the trip. She left us the money the last time she visited us, which was the fourth visit she has made since I left South Africa.

On her second visit, Gertrude brought a wheelchair for Peter. She had been disturbed on her first visit by the way he was living, and knew we didn't have the money to get him a wheelchair. She went back and raised the money for the wheelchair with the help of Happiness, Titus, Wellington, Mazvita, Rachel and Muzhindu.

Now they have all put money together for our travel expenses to South Africa. If Esther and Peter fall in love with South Africa, and we can stay there legally, there is a high probability that we will never return to Zimbabwe.

ND - #0475 - 270225 - C0 - 229/152/21 - PB - 9781909544253 - Matt Lamination